metrix

EST PREPARATION

I0891997

tate

rooper

xam Secrets

tudy Guide

Dear Future Exam Success Story

First of all, **THANK YOU** for purchasing Mometrix study materials!

Second, congratulations! You are one of the few determined test-takers who are committed to doing whatever it takes to excel on your exam. **You have come to the right place.** We developed these study materials with one goal in mind: to deliver you the information you need in a format that's concise and easy to use.

In addition to optimizing your guide for the content of the test, we've outlined our recommended steps for breaking down the preparation process into small, attainable goals so you can make sure you stay on track.

We've also analyzed the entire test-taking process, identifying the most common pitfalls and showing how you can overcome them and be ready for any curveball the test throws you.

Standardized testing is one of the biggest obstacles on your road to success, which only increases the importance of doing well in the high-pressure, high-stakes environment of test day. Your results on this test could have a significant impact on your future, and this guide provides the information and practical advice to help you achieve your full potential on test day.

Your success is our success

We would love to hear from you! If you would like to share the story of your exam success or if you have any questions or comments in regard to our products, please contact us at **800-673-8175** or **support@mometrix.com**.

Thanks again for your business and we wish you continued success!

Sincerely,
The Mometrix Test Preparation Team

Written and edited by the Mometrix Exam Secrets Test Prep Team
Printed in the United States of America

TABLE OF CONTENTS

Introduction

Thank you for purchasing this resource! You have made the choice to prepare yourself for a test that could have a huge impact on your future, and this guide is designed to help you be fully ready for test day. Obviously, it's important to have a solid understanding of the test material, but you also need to be prepared for the unique environment and stressors of the test, so that you can perform to the best of your abilities.

For this purpose, the first section that appears in this guide is the **Secret Keys**. We've devoted countless hours to meticulously researching what works and what doesn't, and we've boiled down our findings to the five most impactful steps you can take to improve your performance on the test. We start at the beginning with study planning and move through the preparation process, all the way to the testing strategies that will help you get the most out of what you know when you're finally sitting in front of the test.

We recommend that you start preparing for your test as far in advance as possible. However, if you've bought this guide as a last-minute study resource and only have a few days before your test, we recommend that you skip over the first two Secret Keys since they address a long-term study plan.

If you struggle with **test anxiety**, we strongly encourage you to check out our recommendations for how you can overcome it. Test anxiety is a formidable foe, but it can be beaten, and we want to make sure you have the tools you need to defeat it.

Secret Key 1: Plan Big, Study Small

There's a lot riding on your performance. If you want to ace this test, you're going to need to keep your skills sharp and the material fresh in your mind. You need a plan that lets you review everything you need to know while still fitting in your schedule. We'll break this strategy down into three categories.

Information Organization

Start with the information you already have: the official test outline. From this, you can make a complete list of all the concepts you need to cover before the test. Organize these concepts into groups that can be studied together, and create a list of any related vocabulary you need to learn so you can brush up on any difficult terms. You'll want to keep this vocabulary list handy once you actually start studying since you may need to add to it along the way.

Time Management

Once you have your set of study concepts, decide how to spread them out over the time you have left before the test. Break your study plan into small, clear goals so you have a manageable task for each day and know exactly what you're doing. Then just focus on one small step at a time. When you manage your time this way, you don't need to spend hours at a time studying. Studying a small block of content for a short period each day helps you retain information better and avoid stressing over how much you have left to do. You can relax knowing that you have a plan to cover everything in time. In order for this strategy to be effective though, you have to start studying early and stick to your schedule. Avoid the exhaustion and futility that comes from last-minute cramming!

Study Environment

The environment you study in has a big impact on your learning. Studying in a coffee shop, while probably more enjoyable, is not likely to be as fruitful as studying in a quiet room. It's important to keep distractions to a minimum. You're only planning to study for a short block of time, so make the most of it. Don't pause to check your phone or get up to find a snack. It's also important to **avoid multitasking**. Research has consistently shown that multitasking will make your studying dramatically less effective. Your study area should also be comfortable and well-lit so you don't have the distraction of straining your eyes or sitting on an uncomfortable chair.

The time of day you study is also important. You want to be rested and alert. Don't wait until just before bedtime. Study when you'll be most likely to comprehend and remember. Even better, if you know what time of day your test will be, set that time aside for study. That way your brain will be used to working on that subject at that specific time and you'll have a better chance of recalling information.

Finally, it can be helpful to team up with others who are studying for the same test. Your actual studying should be done in as isolated an environment as possible, but the work of organizing the information and setting up the study plan can be divided up. In between study sessions, you can discuss with your teammates the concepts that you're all studying and quiz each other on the details. Just be sure that your teammates are as serious about the test as you are. If you find that your study time is being replaced with social time, you might need to find a new team.

Secret Key 2: Make Your Studying Count

You're devoting a lot of time and effort to preparing for this test, so you want to be absolutely certain it will pay off. This means doing more than just reading the content and hoping you can remember it on test day. It's important to make every minute of study count. There are two main areas you can focus on to make your studying count.

Retention

It doesn't matter how much time you study if you can't remember the material. You need to make sure you are retaining the concepts. To check your retention of the information you're learning, try recalling it at later times with minimal prompting. Try carrying around flashcards and glance at one or two from time to time or ask a friend who's also studying for the test to quiz you.

To enhance your retention, look for ways to put the information into practice so that you can apply it rather than simply recalling it. If you're using the information in practical ways, it will be much easier to remember. Similarly, it helps to solidify a concept in your mind if you're not only reading it to yourself but also explaining it to someone else. Ask a friend to let you teach them about a concept you're a little shaky on (or speak aloud to an imaginary audience if necessary). As you try to summarize, define, give examples, and answer your friend's questions, you'll understand the concepts better and they will stay with you longer. Finally, step back for a big picture view and ask yourself how each piece of information fits with the whole subject. When you link the different concepts together and see them working together as a whole, it's easier to remember the individual components.

Finally, practice showing your work on any multi-step problems, even if you're just studying. Writing out each step you take to solve a problem will help solidify the process in your mind, and you'll be more likely to remember it during the test.

Modality

Modality simply refers to the means or method by which you study. Choosing a study modality that fits your own individual learning style is crucial. No two people learn best in exactly the same way, so it's important to know your strengths and use them to your advantage.

For example, if you learn best by visualization, focus on visualizing a concept in your mind and draw an image or a diagram. Try color-coding your notes, illustrating them, or creating symbols that will trigger your mind to recall a learned concept. If you learn best by hearing or discussing information, find a study partner who learns the same way or read aloud to yourself. Think about how to put the information in your own words. Imagine that you are giving a lecture on the topic and record yourself so you can listen to it later.

For any learning style, flashcards can be helpful. Organize the information so you can take advantage of spare moments to review. Underline key words or phrases. Use different colors for different categories. Mnemonic devices (such as creating a short list in which every item starts with the same letter) can also help with retention. Find what works best for you and use it to store the information in your mind most effectively and easily.

Secret Key 3: Practice the Right Way

Your success on test day depends not only on how many hours you put into preparing, but also on whether you prepared the right way. It's good to check along the way to see if your studying is paying off. One of the most effective ways to do this is by taking practice tests to evaluate your progress. Practice tests are useful because they show exactly where you need to improve. Every time you take a practice test, pay special attention to these three groups of questions:

- The questions you got wrong
- The questions you had to guess on, even if you guessed right
- The questions you found difficult or slow to work through

This will show you exactly what your weak areas are, and where you need to devote more study time. Ask yourself why each of these questions gave you trouble. Was it because you didn't understand the material? Was it because you didn't remember the vocabulary? Do you need more repetitions on this type of question to build speed and confidence? Dig into those questions and figure out how you can strengthen your weak areas as you go back to review the material.

Additionally, many practice tests have a section explaining the answer choices. It can be tempting to read the explanation and think that you now have a good understanding of the concept. However, an explanation likely only covers part of the question's broader context. Even if the explanation makes perfect sense, **go back and investigate** every concept related to the question until you're positive you have a thorough understanding.

As you go along, keep in mind that the practice test is just that: practice. Memorizing these questions and answers will not be very helpful on the actual test because it is unlikely to have any of the same exact questions. If you only know the right answers to the sample questions, you won't be prepared for the real thing. **Study the concepts** until you understand them fully, and then you'll be able to answer any question that shows up on the test.

It's important to wait on the practice tests until you're ready. If you take a test on your first day of study, you may be overwhelmed by the amount of material covered and how much you need to learn. Work up to it gradually.

On test day, you'll need to be prepared for answering questions, managing your time, and using the test-taking strategies you've learned. It's a lot to balance, like a mental marathon that will have a big impact on your future. Like training for a marathon, you'll need to start slowly and work your way up. When test day arrives, you'll be ready.

Start with the strategies you've read in the first two Secret Keys—plan your course and study in the way that works best for you. If you have time, consider using multiple study resources to get different approaches to the same concepts. It can be helpful to see difficult concepts from more than one angle. Then find a good source for practice tests. Many times, the test website will suggest potential study resources or provide sample tests.

Practice Test Strategy

If you're able to find at least three practice tests, we recommend this strategy:

Untimed and Open-Book Practice

Take the first test with no time constraints and with your notes and study guide handy. Take your time and focus on applying the strategies you've learned.

Timed and Open-Book Practice

Take the second practice test open-book as well, but set a timer and practice pacing yourself to finish in time.

Timed and Closed-Book Practice

Take any other practice tests as if it were test day. Set a timer and put away your study materials. Sit at a table or desk in a quiet room, imagine yourself at the testing center, and answer questions as quickly and accurately as possible.

Keep repeating timed and closed-book tests on a regular basis until you run out of practice tests or it's time for the actual test. Your mind will be ready for the schedule and stress of test day, and you'll be able to focus on recalling the material you've learned.

Secret Key 4: Pace Yourself

Once you're fully prepared for the material on the test, your biggest challenge on test day will be managing your time. Just knowing that the clock is ticking can make you panic even if you have plenty of time left. Work on pacing yourself so you can build confidence against the time constraints of the exam. Pacing is a difficult skill to master, especially in a high-pressure environment, so **practice is vital**.

Set time expectations for your pace based on how much time is available. For example, if a section has 60 questions and the time limit is 30 minutes, you know you have to average 30 seconds or less per question in order to answer them all. Although 30 seconds is the hard limit, set 25 seconds per question as your goal, so you reserve extra time to spend on harder questions. When you budget extra time for the harder questions, you no longer have any reason to stress when those questions take longer to answer.

Don't let this time expectation distract you from working through the test at a calm, steady pace, but keep it in mind so you don't spend too much time on any one question. Recognize that taking extra time on one question you don't understand may keep you from answering two that you do understand later in the test. If your time limit for a question is up and you're still not sure of the answer, mark it and move on, and come back to it later if the time and the test format allow. If the testing format doesn't allow you to return to earlier questions, just make an educated guess; then put it out of your mind and move on.

On the easier questions, be careful not to rush. It may seem wise to hurry through them so you have more time for the challenging ones, but it's not worth missing one if you know the concept and just didn't take the time to read the question fully. Work efficiently but make sure you understand the question and have looked at all of the answer choices, since more than one may seem right at first.

Even if you're paying attention to the time, you may find yourself a little behind at some point. You should speed up to get back on track, but do so wisely. Don't panic; just take a few seconds less on each question until you're caught up. Don't guess without thinking, but do look through the answer choices and eliminate any you know are wrong. If you can get down to two choices, it is often worthwhile to guess from those. Once you've chosen an answer, move on and don't dwell on any that you skipped or had to hurry through. If a question was taking too long, chances are it was one of the harder ones, so you weren't as likely to get it right anyway.

On the other hand, if you find yourself getting ahead of schedule, it may be beneficial to slow down a little. The more quickly you work, the more likely you are to make a careless mistake that will affect your score. You've budgeted time for each question, so don't be afraid to spend that time. Practice an efficient but careful pace to get the most out of the time you have.

Secret Key 5: Have a Plan for Guessing

When you're taking the test, you may find yourself stuck on a question. Some of the answer choices seem better than others, but you don't see the one answer choice that is obviously correct. What do you do?

The scenario described above is very common, yet most test takers have not effectively prepared for it. Developing and practicing a plan for guessing may be one of the single most effective uses of your time as you get ready for the exam.

In developing your plan for guessing, there are three questions to address:

- When should you start the guessing process?
- How should you narrow down the choices?
- Which answer should you choose?

When to Start the Guessing Process

Unless your plan for guessing is to select C every time (which, despite its merits, is not what we recommend), you need to leave yourself enough time to apply your answer elimination strategies. Since you have a limited amount of time for each question, that means that if you're going to give yourself the best shot at guessing correctly, you have to decide quickly whether or not you will guess.

Of course, the best-case scenario is that you don't have to guess at all, so first, see if you can answer the question based on your knowledge of the subject and basic reasoning skills. Focus on the key words in the question and try to jog your memory of related topics. Give yourself a chance to bring the knowledge to mind, but once you realize that you don't have (or you can't access) the knowledge you need to answer the question, it's time to start the guessing process.

It's almost always better to start the guessing process too early than too late. It only takes a few seconds to remember something and answer the question from knowledge. Carefully eliminating wrong answer choices takes longer. Plus, going through the process of eliminating answer choices can actually help jog your memory.

Summary: Start the guessing process as soon as you decide that you can't answer the question based on your knowledge.

How to Narrow Down the Choices

The next chapter in this book (**Test-Taking Strategies**) includes a wide range of strategies for how to approach questions and how to look for answer choices to eliminate. You will definitely want to read those carefully, practice them, and figure out which ones work best for you. Here though, we're going to address a mindset rather than a particular strategy.

Your odds of guessing an answer correctly depend on how many options you are choosing from.

Number of options left	5	4	3	2	1
Odds of guessing correctly	20%	25%	33%	50%	100%

You can see from this chart just how valuable it is to be able to eliminate incorrect answers and make an educated guess, but there are two things that many test takers do that cause them to miss out on the benefits of guessing:

- Accidentally eliminating the correct answer
- Selecting an answer based on an impression

We'll look at the first one here, and the second one in the next section.

To avoid accidentally eliminating the correct answer, we recommend a thought exercise called **the $5 challenge**. In this challenge, you only eliminate an answer choice from contention if you are willing to bet $5 on it being wrong. Why $5? Five dollars is a small but not insignificant amount of money. It's an amount you could afford to lose but wouldn't want to throw away. And while losing $5 once might not hurt too much, doing it twenty times will set you back $100. In the same way, each small decision you make—eliminating a choice here, guessing on a question there—won't by itself impact your score very much, but when you put them all together, they can make a big difference. By holding each answer choice elimination decision to a higher standard, you can reduce the risk of accidentally eliminating the correct answer.

The $5 challenge can also be applied in a positive sense: If you are willing to bet $5 that an answer choice *is* correct, go ahead and mark it as correct.

Summary: Only eliminate an answer choice if you are willing to bet $5 that it is wrong.

Which Answer to Choose

You're taking the test. You've run into a hard question and decided you'll have to guess. You've eliminated all the answer choices you're willing to bet $5 on. Now you have to pick an answer. Why do we even need to talk about this? Why can't you just pick whichever one you feel like when the time comes?

The answer to these questions is that if you don't come into the test with a plan, you'll rely on your impression to select an answer choice, and if you do that, you risk falling into a trap. The test writers know that everyone who takes their test will be guessing on some of the questions, so they intentionally write wrong answer choices to seem plausible. You still have to pick an answer though, and if the wrong answer choices are designed to look right, how can you ever be sure that you're not falling for their trap? The best solution we've found to this dilemma is to take the decision out of your hands entirely. Here is the process we recommend:

Once you've eliminated any choices that you are confident (willing to bet $5) are wrong, select the first remaining choice as your answer.

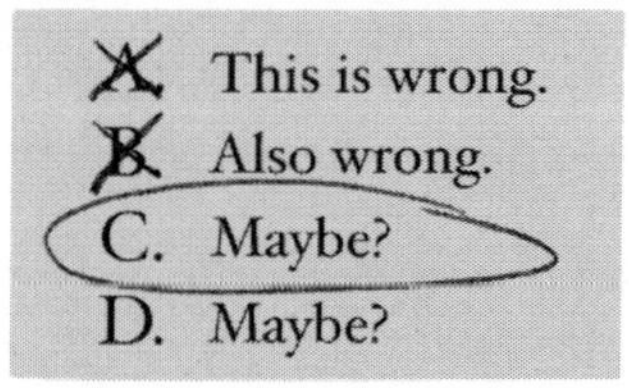

Whether you choose to select the first remaining choice, the second, or the last, the important thing is that you use some preselected standard. Using this approach guarantees that you will not be enticed into selecting an answer choice that looks right, because you are not basing your decision on how the answer choices look.

This is not meant to make you question your knowledge. Instead, it is to help you recognize the difference between your knowledge and your impressions. There's a huge difference between thinking an answer is right because of what you know, and thinking an answer is right because it looks or sounds like it should be right.

Summary: To ensure that your selection is appropriately random, make a predetermined selection from among all answer choices you have not eliminated.

Test-Taking Strategies

This section contains a list of test-taking strategies that you may find helpful as you work through the test. By taking what you know and applying logical thought, you can maximize your chances of answering any question correctly!

It is very important to realize that every question is different and every person is different: no single strategy will work on every question, and no single strategy will work for every person. That's why we've included all of them here, so you can try them out and determine which ones work best for different types of questions and which ones work best for you.

Question Strategies

✓ Read Carefully

Read the question and the answer choices carefully. Don't miss the question because you misread the terms. You have plenty of time to read each question thoroughly and make sure you understand what is being asked. Yet a happy medium must be attained, so don't waste too much time. You must read carefully and efficiently.

✓ Contextual Clues

Look for contextual clues. If the question includes a word you are not familiar with, look at the immediate context for some indication of what the word might mean. Contextual clues can often give you all the information you need to decipher the meaning of an unfamiliar word. Even if you can't determine the meaning, you may be able to narrow down the possibilities enough to make a solid guess at the answer to the question.

✓ Prefixes

If you're having trouble with a word in the question or answer choices, try dissecting it. Take advantage of every clue that the word might include. Prefixes can be a huge help. Usually, they allow you to determine a basic meaning. *Pre-* means before, *post-* means after, *pro-* is positive, *de-* is negative. From prefixes, you can get an idea of the general meaning of the word and try to put it into context.

✓ Hedge Words

Watch out for critical hedge words, such as *likely, may, can, often, almost, mostly, usually, generally, rarely,* and *sometimes.* Question writers insert these hedge phrases to cover every possibility. Often an answer choice will be wrong simply because it leaves no room for exception. Be on guard for answer choices that have definitive words such as *exactly* and *always.*

✓ Switchback Words

Stay alert for *switchbacks*. These are the words and phrases frequently used to alert you to shifts in thought. The most common switchback words are *but, although*, and *however*. Others include *nevertheless, on the other hand, even though, while, in spite of, despite*, and *regardless of*. Switchback words are important to catch because they can change the direction of the question or an answer choice.

✓ Face Value

When in doubt, use common sense. Accept the situation in the problem at face value. Don't read too much into it. These problems will not require you to make wild assumptions. If you have to go beyond creativity and warp time or space in order to have an answer choice fit the question, then you should move on and consider the other answer choices. These are normal problems rooted in reality. The applicable relationship or explanation may not be readily apparent, but it is there for you to figure out. Use your common sense to interpret anything that isn't clear.

Answer Choice Strategies

✓ Answer Selection

The most thorough way to pick an answer choice is to identify and eliminate wrong answers until only one is left, then confirm it is the correct answer. Sometimes an answer choice may immediately seem right, but be careful. The test writers will usually put more than one reasonable answer choice on each question, so take a second to read all of them and make sure that the other choices are not equally obvious. As long as you have time left, it is better to read every answer choice than to pick the first one that looks right without checking the others.

✓ Answer Choice Families

An answer choice family consists of two (in rare cases, three) answer choices that are very similar in construction and cannot all be true at the same time. If you see two answer choices that are direct opposites or parallels, one of them is usually the correct answer. For instance, if one answer choice says that quantity *x* increases and another either says that quantity *x* decreases (opposite) or says that quantity *y* increases (parallel), then those answer choices would fall into the same family. An answer choice that doesn't match the construction of the answer choice family is more likely to be incorrect. Most questions will not have answer choice families, but when they do appear, you should be prepared to recognize them.

✓ Eliminate Answers

Eliminate answer choices as soon as you realize they are wrong, but make sure you consider all possibilities. If you are eliminating answer choices and realize that the last one you are left with is also wrong, don't panic. Start over and consider each choice again. There may be something you missed the first time that you will realize on the second pass.

⊘ Avoid Fact Traps

Don't be distracted by an answer choice that is factually true but doesn't answer the question. You are looking for the choice that answers the question. Stay focused on what the question is asking for so you don't accidentally pick an answer that is true but incorrect. Always go back to the question and make sure the answer choice you've selected actually answers the question and is not merely a true statement.

⊘ Extreme Statements

In general, you should avoid answers that put forth extreme actions as standard practice or proclaim controversial ideas as established fact. An answer choice that states the "process should be used in certain situations, if..." is much more likely to be correct than one that states the "process should be discontinued completely." The first is a calm rational statement and doesn't even make a definitive, uncompromising stance, using a hedge word *if* to provide wiggle room, whereas the second choice is far more extreme.

⊘ Benchmark

As you read through the answer choices and you come across one that seems to answer the question well, mentally select that answer choice. This is not your final answer, but it's the one that will help you evaluate the other answer choices. The one that you selected is your benchmark or standard for judging each of the other answer choices. Every other answer choice must be compared to your benchmark. That choice is correct until proven otherwise by another answer choice beating it. If you find a better answer, then that one becomes your new benchmark. Once you've decided that no other choice answers the question as well as your benchmark, you have your final answer.

⊘ Predict the Answer

Before you even start looking at the answer choices, it is often best to try to predict the answer. When you come up with the answer on your own, it is easier to avoid distractions and traps because you will know exactly what to look for. The right answer choice is unlikely to be word-for-word what you came up with, but it should be a close match. Even if you are confident that you have the right answer, you should still take the time to read each option before moving on.

General Strategies

⊘ Tough Questions

If you are stumped on a problem or it appears too hard or too difficult, don't waste time. Move on! Remember though, if you can quickly check for obviously incorrect answer choices, your chances of guessing correctly are greatly improved. Before you completely give up, at least try to knock out a couple of possible answers. Eliminate what you can and then guess at the remaining answer choices before moving on.

✓ Check Your Work

Since you will probably not know every term listed and the answer to every question, it is important that you get credit for the ones that you do know. Don't miss any questions through careless mistakes. If at all possible, try to take a second to look back over your answer selection and make sure you've selected the correct answer choice and haven't made a costly careless mistake (such as marking an answer choice that you didn't mean to mark). This quick double check should more than pay for itself in caught mistakes for the time it costs.

✓ Pace Yourself

It's easy to be overwhelmed when you're looking at a page full of questions; your mind is confused and full of random thoughts, and the clock is ticking down faster than you would like. Calm down and maintain the pace that you have set for yourself. Especially as you get down to the last few minutes of the test, don't let the small numbers on the clock make you panic. As long as you are on track by monitoring your pace, you are guaranteed to have time for each question.

✓ Don't Rush

It is very easy to make errors when you are in a hurry. Maintaining a fast pace in answering questions is pointless if it makes you miss questions that you would have gotten right otherwise. Test writers like to include distracting information and wrong answers that seem right. Taking a little extra time to avoid careless mistakes can make all the difference in your test score. Find a pace that allows you to be confident in the answers that you select.

✓ Keep Moving

Panicking will not help you pass the test, so do your best to stay calm and keep moving. Taking deep breaths and going through the answer elimination steps you practiced can help to break through a stress barrier and keep your pace.

Final Notes

The combination of a solid foundation of content knowledge and the confidence that comes from practicing your plan for applying that knowledge is the key to maximizing your performance on test day. As your foundation of content knowledge is built up and strengthened, you'll find that the strategies included in this chapter become more and more effective in helping you quickly sift through the distractions and traps of the test to isolate the correct answer.

Now that you're preparing to move forward into the test content chapters of this book, be sure to keep your goal in mind. As you read, think about how you will be able to apply this information on the test. If you've already seen sample questions for the test and you have an idea of the question format and style, try to come up with questions of your own that you can answer based on what you're reading. This will give you valuable practice applying your knowledge in the same ways you can expect to on test day.

Good luck and good studying!

Introduction

Congratulations! You have decided to take one of the state trooper examinations, which means you are pursuing employment as a law enforcement officer. Becoming a state trooper is a great way to help yourself and your community at the same time. For many aspiring state troopers, however, the application process can be daunting. In order to be admitted to the state trooper training academy, you will need to pass a series of assessments. The state trooper examination program is a battery of written, physical, and interpersonal examinations that determine whether you are qualified to serve as a state trooper. This may sound intimidating, but have no fear: the majority of applicants pass the examinations, and this guidebook can help ensure that you are among that successful majority. The good news about the state trooper examinations is that they require no specialized knowledge of police procedure. You will, however, be required to possess basic knowledge of mathematics and standard written English. More importantly, you will be required to demonstrate common sense and sound judgment. Nevertheless, preparing for the state trooper examinations is a simple matter of diligence and planning; with the information and tips included in this book, you will have all the resources you need to excel!

Format of the Exam

The precise format of the state trooper examination will depend on the state in which you are applying. In some states, the job description of a state trooper is unique and the examination requires different points of emphasis. For the most part, however, the state trooper examinations for all fifty states contain the same basic elements. The entire application process will contain written, physical, psychological, and medical examinations. Many states will require a formal interview and, if you make it to the end of the application process, most states will perform a basic background check on you.

This book will provide comprehensive instruction on the types of questions you are likely to encounter on the written examination. Most state trooper written examinations include questions from the following content areas: reading comprehension, written comprehension, police judgment, orientation (map-reading), and memory. These subjects comprise the basic repertoire of skills required to be a state trooper. The format of these examinations is similar to other standardized tests: they are primarily composed of multiple-choice questions which must be answered within a certain amount of time. The written examination is administered by the state department or by a licensed test administrator. Information regarding testing dates and locations will be given during registration. Your score on the written examination will indicate your ability to meet the mental requirements of the job.

In addition to the written examination, the application process may include a physical assessment, psychological examination, interview, medical exam, and background check. These assessments measure your ability to meet the physical, ethical, and psychological demands of the job. They are usually issued directly by the state department or by organizations working in consultation with the department. In a typical application schedule, these assessments take place after the written examination. Contrary to what you may think, it is possible to prepare for all of these assessments in order to bolster your chances of success; this book contains specific strategies you can use to do so.

How to Use This Book

As noted above, the state trooper examination you are required to take may not include all of the topics covered in this book. So, before you begin using this book to prepare for the exam, you should check with the state department to determine the precise characteristics of the written examination you will be required to take. You may find that it is not necessary for you to read certain parts of the book.

Furthermore, you should not attempt to read this guidebook without interruption. For one thing, you may find that you already have enough knowledge to succeed on parts of the exam. If you are a math expert, for instance, you can feel free to skip our discussion of basic operations with integers; if you are a master of the written word, you may not need to review some of the elementary concepts of punctuation and grammar. Try to focus on the subjects that are unfamiliar and difficult to you, where a little bit of instruction will result in the most progress.

Finally, you should avoid reading this book from start to finish without interruption. Much of the material contained herein is rather dry, and may require multiple readings for full absorption. In addition, much of what is described here is only fully comprehensible through practice. Throughout the book, we have tried to indicate some practice exercises you can use to supplement the information contained in the book. Unless you practice the skills described here, you may have a hard time applying your knowledge on the examination itself. Consider this guidebook as a map you can use to lead yourself toward success on the state trooper examinations.

Reading Comprehension

Purpose

Every state trooper examination will contain some reading comprehension questions. Although critical reading skills are not normally considered to be part of the repertoire of a state trooper, in actuality a trooper is required to read and understand a number of different texts during the course of his or her service. Troopers will need to be able to read and understand legal statutes and case records, so that they can obtain useful information. Especially during training, troopers will need to be able to read and understand law enforcement manuals. Occasionally, the trooper will need to read investigative reports on a particular subject. Finally, troopers are often required to read and respond to complaints made by members of the community. As you can see, then, the ability to comprehend and respond to a written text is an essential skill for a state trooper.

Four Basic Types

For most applicants, the reading comprehension questions require the most work. On your exam, you will be asked a number of questions based on passages of a few paragraphs. These passages will pertain to topics related to police work and law enforcement. The reading comprehension exercises on the exam are designed to assess your ability to read carefully, analyze the relationships among different parts of a passage, and draw inferences from the material in the passage. The reading comprehension questions on the exam are of four basic types (main idea, detail, tone, and extending the author's reasoning), each of which calls for a slightly different approach.

Format

The format of reading comprehension questions should not pose any problems. Most of the state trooper exams contain three or four passages of approximately three hundred words (about three paragraphs of four sentences). Each of these passages will be followed by three or four questions. These questions will be in a multiple-choice format, with four or five possible correct answers. For the most part, questions pertaining to the beginning of the passage will come before questions pertaining to the end of the passage. The reading comprehension questions on the exam are meant to be comprehensible to a general audience, and will not contain any specialized jargon. Also, all of the information required to answer the questions will be found in the passages; you will not need any outside information or experience. Now, let's take a quick look at the content of the passages that will appear on the exam.

Subjects

By and large, the reading comprehension passages on state trooper exams are on subjects related to law enforcement. For instance, the passages may describe a particular set of laws or a protocol for police action. Some passages are technical descriptions of the equipment used in the line of duty. Still other passages outline a potentially criminal scenario and ask you to make some observations. The passages may also be more abstract, focusing on the philosophy of criminal justice and law enforcement. You will not need any special knowledge of police work or criminal justice theory to understand the content of the reading comprehension passages; all of the information required to answer the questions will be provided in the passage. However, you may want to spend a little time before the exam looking over some basic texts in criminal justice and law enforcement, just to get a taste of the writing style used in these publications. There are a number of trade journals and basic primers on police work that can be obtained at the public library. In addition, the department in which you are applying for employment will have some relevant texts on hand.

Types of Questions

Now that we have covered the content areas from which the reading comprehension passages will be drawn, let us consider the types of questions that you will encounter. The first and most basic kind of reading comprehension question is the one that asks you to define the main idea of the passage. This question may arrive in any of a few different forms. The question may ask you for the "the best summary," the "salient point," or the "overarching theme" of the passage. Do not be flummoxed by the precise language: this is a main idea question. And, as you no doubt have learned by now, the main idea of a passage is most likely to appear in either the first or the last sentence. So, as you are reading a passage for the first time, pay special attention to the beginning and end. Whether the main idea is offered first or last will depend on the type of passage: expository passages tend to give a main idea first and then spend the rest of the sentences defending it, while critical or argumentative essays will often begin with a set of loose facts and end with a summarizing conclusion. In any case, be prepared to refer back to the text in search of the main idea.

- *Main idea:* On occasion, the authors of the exam will try to fool you by asking you to provide the main idea of a specific *part* of the passage rather than of the passage as a whole. Similarly, they may try to confuse you with answer choices that are true without being the main idea of the passage. For this reason, it is imperative that you read the question carefully and do not just assume that the first or last sentence of the paragraph is the main idea. The main idea is not just any true statement contained within the passage: it is the idea that most effectively summarizes the entire passage. It is certain that at least a couple of the reading comprehension questions will ask you to determine the main idea. In addition, it is quite likely that a few of the questions will ask you to recall specific details from the passage. This would appear to be the easiest kind of question to answer, but many students go astray by relying on memory instead of scrolling back up to find the pertinent details in the passage. Remember that you are free to refer to the text as much as you like. Also, remember that specific questions are likely to have specific answers, just as general questions are likely to have general answers. In other words, if the question asks you to name a concept, the answer probably will not be a piece of specific data.
- *Diagnosing attitude:* A more subtle form of question is the one that requires you to diagnose the author's attitude. As with the main idea question, this kind of question can take a number of different forms. It may ask you to describe the tone, opinion, feeling, or mood of the author or passage. All of these questions are essentially asking you to assess how the author feels about his or her topic. In order to answer such a question, you will have to pay attention to the specific language used by the author, and the point of view that the language conveys. For instance, if the author is describing a small person, he or she would create a sharply different tone by using the word *puny* than by using the word *petite*. *Puny* suggests a shriveled, scrawny individual, while *petite* conjures daintiness and delicacy. It may take a little bit of practice before you habitually notice these shades of meaning, but you should try to be conscious of the ways in which language can be used to subtly indicate attitude. For the most part, the test administrators avoid passages that are violently opinionated or controversial. Any answer choices that suggest the author holds an opinion which could be considered radical or offensive are most likely incorrect.

- *Extend the reasoning:* The final category of question which you may encounter on the exam is one that asks you to extend the author's reasoning. Put another way, these questions require you to consider the information provided in the passage and then use this information to consider a problem not mentioned in the passage. For example, a passage might describe the characteristics of a given community and the police activity that is recommended for that community. A question might then ask you to extend the reasoning of the author by describing the changes in police activity that could be made in response to a change in the community. The reasoning required to answer these kinds of questions will not be extremely complicated. The most common problem students have with questions asking them to extend the reasoning of the passage is that they attempt to find the answer explicitly in the passage. Remember that even though all of the information needed to answer every question can be found in the text, some questions will require you to do some independent thinking.

IMPORTANT PRACTICE

The best way to prepare for the reading comprehension section of the written examination is to practice reading a variety of different texts. By visiting the law enforcement department or the local library, you should be able to obtain journal articles, training manuals, written complaints, and persuasive essays on issues related to law enforcement. As you read these texts, practice finding the main idea and identifying key details. You may want to practice scanning a short passage to determine the basic structure, before you go back and read in more detail. You will be allowed to make notes and underline on the written examination, so feel free to do this during your practice if it helps you to understand the text.

Written Comprehension

Purpose

Unbeknownst to many state trooper applicants, one of the most effective tools of the law enforcement officer is the English language. In order to succeed in the police service, an officer has to be able to compose clear and precise reports that can be understood by a superior officer. Officers are also required to fill out deposition forms on a regular basis, and their entries on these forms need to be direct and comprehensible. State troopers do not have to be elegant or flowery writers, but they need to be able to express themselves with precision and detail. For this reason, every state trooper examination contains some exercises designed to test linguistic skills.

Target

Written comprehension questions specifically target your command of the English language and the norms of standard written English. Some written comprehension questions will test your knowledge of specific rules of grammar, while others will gauge your ability to notice errors of style or tone in a sentence. Do not be alarmed if you do not remember your grammar instruction from high school! The test administrator wishes to avoid controversy, so it limits the written comprehension questions on the exam to a few clear and basic rules of style and grammar. After taking a quick look at the format of the written comprehension questions, we will cover all of the content you will need for this portion of the exam.

Format

There are a couple of different formats for written comprehension questions. One type of question presents you with four sentences and asks you to select the one that is grammatically incorrect. These sentences may all be saying basically the same thing, or they may be saying completely different things. Another type of question may present you with a sentence and ask you to choose the answer that best expresses the information in the sentence. Several of the answer choices may be grammatically correct; you will be required to choose the one that is most fluent and clear.

Approach

Your approach to written comprehension exercises should be simple: read the original sentence carefully, mentally consider each of the answer choices, eliminate wrong answers, and confirm your judgment by reading to yourself the selected sentence. You should be able to articulate a reason for eliminating or selecting a given answer choice.

Limited Linguistic Issues

Remember that written comprehension questions will not concern issues of vocabulary or slang. In some cases, the correct answer choice will produce a sentence that remains awkward or inelegant; remember that you are looking for the best sentence, not the perfect sentence. Other times, more than one answer choice will produce a sentence that is grammatically correct. If this is the case, try to determine which of the new sentences is more fluent. The good news about written comprehension questions is that they only cover a limited number of linguistic topics. Indeed, when making the written comprehension questions, the test administrator refers to a short list of structural and grammatical issues, which we will now cover in some detail.

Basic Punctuation

Most of the written comprehension questions on the state trooper exam will test your knowledge of basic punctuation. The language of police reports and depositions is ideally clear and concise. For the most part, there is no need for complicated sentence structures and fancy vocabulary. The most important aspect of a state trooper's written expression is clarity. So, in order to make sure that your writing will be comprehensible to your coworkers and other concerned parties, take a moment to refresh your knowledge of the basic elements of punctuation.

Period: The period is the most common punctuation mark used at the end of a sentence. It is placed at the end of any sentence that is not a direct question or an exclamation. Periods are also placed at the end of abbreviations like Mr., Dr., and Ave. It is not necessary to place a period at the end of the abbreviation of a state name (for example, NC or ME). On an exam, you are most likely to see errors in which a period has been placed at the end of a sentence that requires a question mark or exclamation point.

Question mark: The question mark is placed at the end of any direct question (for example: *Where are you going?*). A direct question is one that is being asked by the speaker; an indirect question, on the other hand, is one that is being reported by the speaker (for instance, He asked her where she was going.) Indirect questions do not require question marks.

Exclamation point: The exclamation point is placed after any sentence or phrase that requires special emphasis. Exclamation points are almost never used in police reports, so it is unlikely that they will appear on the state trooper examination.

Comma: The comma is perhaps the trickiest mark of punctuation; it is used in a number of different situations to clarify the meaning of a sentence. When a sentence contains more than one independent clause (that is, more than one group of words that could function as a sentence by itself), a comma is placed before the coordinating conjunction separating the clauses. Coordinating conjunctions are words like *and*, *but*, *or*, and *so* that are used to demonstrate the relationship between the two independent clauses. An example of this kind of comma use is found in the following sentence: *Dave dressed for the dance, but Roger still had not arrived with his corsage.*

- Commas are also placed after the introductory word phrase in a sentence. An introductory word phrase can be an adverb, participial phrase, or transitional phrase. An example of this comma use is the following: *After Henry began to eat, his dog barked at the front door.* Obviously, if this sentence did not contain a comma after *eat* the meaning would be much different! This is a good general rule of thumb regarding commas: they are required when they enable the sentence to be understood as meaning what it was intended to mean.
- Commas should also be placed between all of the items in a series or list, as for instance in the following sentence: *The shopping list included eggs, milk, and bread.* Although some writers omit the final comma in a list of this kind, grammarians insist that it should be included to minimize confusion.
- Commas are also used to set aside nonrestrictive elements in a sentence. A nonrestrictive element is one that refers to a noun or pronoun which has already been sufficiently defined. As an example, consider the following sentence: *Jessica needed to buy a more efficient car, which would be expensive.* The phrase which would be expensive is considered a nonrestrictive element because its omission would not radically alter the meaning of the sentence. For this reason, it is appropriate to set it aside with a comma. A restrictive element, on the other hand, is more integral to the meaning of the sentence: *Jessica needed to buy a car that was more fuel-efficient.* The removal of the phrase *that was more fuel-efficient* would result in a vastly different sentence. In general, commas are used to set aside parenthetical, nonessential, or nonrestrictive information.
- There are also some specialized uses of the comma in the writing of places, dates, and titles. Commas are used to separate the elements of an address: *311 Somerset Road, London, England.* They are also used to set aside the year in the writing of a date: *He was born July 6, 1995.* Finally, commas are used to set aside honorifics and titles, as for instance *John Gibson, M.D.*
- Comma usage is complicated and somewhat intuitive. The above information summarizes the basic functions of a comma, but there are other situations in which a comma would be appropriate. Perhaps the best way to learn correct comma usage is to pay attention to how they are used in the books and articles you read. You will no doubt notice that the use of commas varies between writers. In general, though, the predominant purpose of the comma is to preserve the sense of the sentence; so, when you encounter questionable comma usage on the exam, ask yourself whether the addition or subtraction of a comma would improve the clarity of the expression.

Semi-colon: The semi-colon is another tricky punctuation mark, although it is used much less frequently than the comma. Semi-colons are most often used to separate two related but independent clauses that are not connected with a coordinating conjunction, as in the following sentence: *John never went to see the doctor; his leg improved slowly but steadily in the next week.* This use of a semi-colon is rather advanced grammatically, so it is unlikely that you will need to use it in a police report. Consequently, it is unlikely to appear on the state trooper exam. It is more likely that you will see the semi-colon used to separate the items in a list when those items require internal punctuation. As an example, consider the following sentence: *The recipe called for eggs; vinegar; bread, both white and whole-wheat; and salt.* Because there is a comma after *bread*, the semi-colon is more effective than the comma at setting apart the items in the list.

Colon: The colon, meanwhile, is primarily used before some important or summarizing statement, as in the following sentence: *Dr. Harris walked in and confirmed what we were all guessing: Vincent was dead.* The colon is also used to introduce lists, as in the following sentence: *Ronald immediately sat down and began on his homework: thirty pages of English literature, a few geometry problems, and the abstract to a physics experiment.* Note that the colon functions somewhat as a verb, telling you what the list "is." For this reason, it is not appropriate to use a colon in this manner immediately after a verb. It is appropriate, however, to use a colon immediately after a verb to introduce a list, as in: *Remember what F. Scott Fitzgerald said: "Living well is the best revenge."* Colons can also be used instead of commas after the greeting in a letter, as in *Dear Mother:*

Apostrophe: The apostrophe is used in a few different ways. It is used in combination with an *s* to indicate possession. If the word ends in an *s* already, the apostrophe is placed after the *s*; otherwise, the apostrophe is placed immediately before the *s*. It is important to remember that apostrophes are not used in the following possessive pronouns: *its, hers, his, whose, ours, yours, and theirs.* Another use of the apostrophe is in contractions like *don't, shouldn't*, and *can't.* Note that the apostrophe is placed where the omitted letters would appear. An apostrophe is often used to indicate plurality of numbers, letters, or abbreviations, as in the following: *Dave got 95's on all three of his quizzes; these A's, however, did not pull up his low test scores.* An apostrophe is not used when referring to a decade, as for example the 30s or the 1990s.

Quotation mark: Quotation marks are used to indicate direct quotations of spoken or written language. Quotation marks should not be placed around an indirect quotation, as in the following sentence: *The dentist told me to brush my teeth a bit more vigorously*. When there is a quotation within a quotation, use single quotation marks for the inner quotation: *"My grandmother used to say, 'Never count your chickens before they're hatched,'" Hank recollected.* Quotation marks are used in a few other ways. They are placed around the titles of poems, short stories, songs, and book chapters. (Longer works like novels, books, and albums are placed in italics.) Quotations can also be used in when a word is mentioned as a word, as in the following: *The word "demonstrate" bears no relation to the word "demon."*

Punctuation Placement

On the state trooper exam, you will probably see at least one question pertaining to the placement of other punctuation marks in relation to a set of quotes. Periods and commas should always be placed inside of quotation marks: *"Put your hands up," the robber said. "This is a robbery!"* Colons and semi-colons, on the other hand, should be placed outside of the quotation marks. Question marks and exclamation points should be placed inside the quotation marks if they apply to a direct quotation and outside the quotation marks if they do not.

Capitalization

Occasionally, an exam question will hinge on whether a certain word should be capitalized. Proper nouns (the names of specific persons, places, and things) should always be capitalized. Common nouns are not capitalized. So *Uncle Dave* is capitalized, but *my uncle* is not. Some of the proper nouns likely to appear on the state trooper exam include the names of organizations, political parties, nationalities, languages, departments, and educational institutions. The title of a person is only capitalized when the person's name is given. So, for instance, *Principal Jackson* is capitalized and *school administrator* is not. All the major words in a book title, song title, article title, or other work should be capitalized; major words include everything besides articles, prepositions, and conjunctions. Finally, capitalize the first word of a quoted sentence, as in: *Adam Smith declared, "There is an invisible hand that governs the economy."* However, do not capitalize the first word of a quote that is blended into the sentence: *Adam Smith said that "there is an invisible hand that governs the economy."*

Double Negatives

There are very few situations in which it is appropriate to use two negative words in a sentence. (Negative words are both those that begin with *un-* or *non-* and words like *not, never, nothing*, and *none*). This is mainly because multiple negatives tend to confuse meaning. So, the sentence "*It wasn't not a good day*" should be corrected to read "*It was a good day*." A sentence should never be left with more than one negative. The words *hardly, barely*, and *scarcely* are also considered negatives, so a sentence like "*I can't hardly feel my feet*" should be corrected to "*I can hardly feel my feet*" or "*I can't feel my feet*."

Sentence Fragments

A sentence fragment is one of the easiest errors to spot. Sentences are considered fragments when they are missing either a subject or a predicate. For instance, look at the following fragment: *General Davis, having learned about the possible ambush.* There is a subject (General Davis) and a supporting clause, but there is no predicate telling us what he did with the information he learned. Remember that just because a sentence has a verb does not mean that it has a predicate. The verb must be in agreement with the subject. Because sentence fragments are fairly easy to spot, the exam will often try to camouflage them by making them extremely long. Remember that no matter how many words it contains, it is a sentence fragment if it does not contain both a subject and a predicate.

Parallel Construction Error

When two or more words or phrases are being placed in the same grammatical position in a sentence, they are said to be parallel. Words or phrases that are parallel need to receive the same grammatical treatment. Several of the written comprehension exercises on the exam will concern the two main forms of parallel construction: lists and correlatives. When a sentence contains a list, all of the items in the list need to receive the same grammatical treatment. As an example, read the following sentence: *Andrew had all the symptoms of influenza: headache, fever, and he was nauseous.* Notice how the first two items in the list are simply named, while the last item includes the words *he was.* A grammatically-correct version of this list would read: *headache, fever, and nausea.* Of course, it would also be possible to correct the list as follows: *he had a headache, he had a fever, and he was nauseous.* This is a more awkward wording, but it is a consistent parallel construction. The essential point about parallel constructions is that they must be consistent for all of the items in a list.

The second way in which parallel constructions will be covered on the exam is linked with correlatives. Ideas that are parallel in a sentence must be given the same grammatical treatment. For instance, read the following sentence: *Most people think it is easier to read a book than writing one.* Since the infinitive form *to read* is used in the first part of the sentence, the words *to write* should be substituted for *writing.* Here's another example: *Dr. Baker asked us either to study for the test or wait a week.* The incorrect parallel construction is a little more subtle here, but if the infinitive form *to study* is used then the word *to* should also be inserted before *wait.* Whenever you believe a written comprehension exercise may hinge on an incorrect parallel construction, scan the parallel components of the sentence and determine whether or not they are receiving the same grammatical treatment.

Faulty Comparison

The exam will often contain sentences in which a faulty comparison is made. A faulty comparison exists when the author unintentionally creates a comparison between two unlike ideas or things. Consider the comparison made by the following sentence: *Some people think that the citizens of America are healthier than other countries.* Notice that the author is technically comparing the *citizens of America* with *other countries.* The author's intent is made clear in the corrected sentence. *Some people think that the citizens of America are healthier than the citizens of other countries.* Always make sure that the comparison being made in a sentence is between the right ideas or things.

Adjective/Adverb Error

Once you know what to look for, spotting errors in the use of adjectives and adverbs should be easy. An adjective describes a noun, while an adverb may describe a verb, adjective, or another adverb. In general (but not always), an adverb will end with –*ly.* The written comprehension exercises on the exam will probably include a couple of sentences in which the wrong part of speech is used. For instance, look at the following sentence: *The end of the song was beautifully.* This sentence sounds wrong to the ear, because the adverbial form is inappropriate for modifying the noun phrase *end of the song*. The correct word would be the adjective *beautiful*.

One common exception to the *-ly* rule regarding adverbs involves two adverbs in a row. In such a case, it is typical for the *-ly* to be eliminated from the second adverb. Consider the following sentence: *I didn't feel particularly sadly about the cancelled party*. Even though *particularly* and *sadly* are both adverbs, the sentence is incorrect until the *-ly* is removed from *sadly*: *I didn't feel particularly sad about the cancelled party*.

Personal Pronoun Errors

Personal pronouns are words like *we*, *him*, *it*, and *our*, that substitute for individuals or groups of people. Sometimes in a complicated sentence it can be difficult to determine the appropriate personal pronoun. In order to confidently assert the correct personal pronoun, you need to know the different cases in which a pronoun can be used. The first of these is the subjective case, which includes *I*, *we*, *you*, *he/she/it*, and *they*. These words are used when the pronoun is functioning as the subject of the sentence, as in the following: *Jim and* he *were the winners*. The subjective case is also used when the pronoun is used as a complement to the subject, as in *Steve told us that the winners were Jim and* he, in which *he* is a substitute for *Steve*.

The pronouns *me*, *us*, *you*, *him/her/it*, and *them* are used in the objective case. Pronouns are placed into the objective case when they are used as the direct object, indirect object, or object of a preposition. Here is an example of a pronoun being used as a direct object: *Sarah called Bob and invited* him *to the party*. Here is an example of a pronoun being used as an indirect object: *Yancey gave* me *a wonderful present*. Here is an example of a pronoun being used as the object of a preposition: *Sally decided that the gift must be for* her.

Finally, pronouns may also be used in the possessive case, as in forms like *my*, *our*, *your*, *his/her/its*, and *their*. These are used when the pronoun is establishing ownership of something, as in the sentence *Dave looked high and low for* his *lunch*.

The personal pronoun errors on the exam will usually be pretty obvious. One helpful way to identify a personal pronoun error is to consciously consider the case in which the pronoun is being used. For instance, look at the following sentence: *I can't see anything wrong with you being here*. The pronoun *I* is correct because it is being used as a subject, but *you* actually needs to be in the possessive case *your*, since it describes *your being here*. If you think the sentence may have a personal pronoun error, see if you can pinpoint the exact error of case.

Pronoun-Antecedent Errors

Another way in which pronouns can be used incorrectly is in relation to their antecedents. A pronoun's antecedent is the word to which it refers. A pronoun must always have a clear antecedent, and it must always agree with this antecedent in number. Consider the following sentence: *Darryl and Dirk went to the beach, but he didn't go swimming.* To which person does the pronoun *he* refer? This sentence needs to be corrected to make the tie between pronoun and antecedent clear. A possible correction could be: *Darryl and Dirk went to the beach, but they didn't go swimming.*

Pronouns must also agree with their antecedents in number. Consider the following sentence: *A student must realize that not every teacher will be right for them.* This is actually one of the more common errors in written English: the pronoun *them* is plural, but it refers to a singular *student.* A corrected version of the sentence would read as follows: *A student must realize that not every teacher will be right for him or her.* Whenever you are unsure about pronoun-antecedent agreement, isolate the components and make sure that they have the same number.

Subject and Verb Agreement

The subject and verb in a sentence or clause should always agree in number. This is a fairly basic point of grammar, so the exam will try to disguise disagreement by inserting prepositional phrases between the subject and verb. For instance, read the following sentence: *The group of children with young parents have more life skills than other groups.* Because *have* is placed after *parents*, it almost sounds correct. Remember, though, that the subject and simple predicate (verb) of this sentence is "*The group have,*" which is clearly incorrect. The best way to diagnose disagreement between subject and verb is to eliminate any extra diction and consider the relation of the subject to the simple predicate.

Verb Tense Error

The exam frequently contains errors of verb tense in the written comprehension exercises. Although these mistakes will often be obvious, in some cases they will be hidden by extraneous clauses and prepositional phrases. A good rule of thumb regarding verb tense is that a sentence should maintain the same verb tense throughout. Consider the following sentence: *Dale spent a year in college and had read several books on the subject.* The first verb (*spent*) is in the past tense, while the second (*had read*) is in the past perfect. In order to correct this sentence, the verb tenses need to be made consistent, as in the following: *Dale spent a year in college and read several books on the subject.*

There are some exceptions to the rule of consistency in verb tenses. Occasionally, a sentence will indicate that two or more things are happening at different times, as in the following: *Please tell me when you will mow the grass.* Obviously, the present tense (*tell*) and future tense (*will mow*) are appropriate when the speaker is requesting information about something in the future. So, look for consistency in verb tenses unless the sentence is clearly establishing two different time periods.

Misplaced Modifier

A modifier is any word, phrase, or clause that alters the meaning of another word in the sentence. A modifier can be an adjective, an adverb, or a participial expression. The exam frequently includes sentences with misplaced modifiers. There are a few different ways that modifiers can be misplaced. One common modifier error is when a participial phrase modifies the wrong word, as in: *While looking for the restaurant, John's car got pulled over.* The participial phrase that begins this sentence should modify the first word after the comma; in this construction, the sentence implies that John's car was looking for the restaurant!

Other forms of misplaced modifier error will feature participial phrases, adjectives, and adjectival phrases that modify the wrong noun or pronoun. For instance, read this sentence: *Tender-hearted, the movie brought Fred to tears several times.* Obviously, the sentence means to imply that Fred, not the movie, is tender-hearted. The corrected version would read: *Tender-hearted, Fred was brought to tears several times by the movie.*

Incorrect Idiomatic Expression

One of the trickier areas that the exam occasionally covers is idiomatic expression. This topic is difficult to study because it relies more on an acquired sense of written English than on any consistent rules of grammar. For instance, there is no clear reason why we say that something is *defined as* or *results in*. Surely, it would make no less sense to say *defined of* or *results by,* but these constructions are plainly incorrect. Because idiomatic expression is such a nebulous subject, you should only consider it as a possibility when you have exhausted all of the other possible errors in the sentence. To best get a sense of whether an underlined expression "sounds" right, try isolating it from the rest of the sentence and saying it aloud (quietly, of course!).

Basic Mathematics

Purpose

Those individuals hoping to avoid dealing with math by becoming a state trooper will be disappointed when they sit for the written examination. Although state troopers are not required to perform advanced math in the normal line of duty, there are a number of basic tasks which will require fundamental mathematical understanding. State troopers are often called upon to draw up expense reports, calculate mileages and distances, and calculate fees and bonds. Simply issuing a speeding ticket will require you to determine the amount by which the driver was exceeding the limit. For all of these reasons, the state trooper written examination will contain a few questions testing your basic mathematics skills. These questions primarily pertain to arithmetic, though there may be some questions which require knowledge of basic algebra and geometry. The level of difficulty is approximately that of a sophomore- or junior-year math class in high school. So, with a little bit of a refresher, you should have no problem with this section of the exam.

Format

The format of the basic mathematics questions should be familiar to you from other standardized tests. You will be asked to solve a problem, find the value of a variable, or provide some other piece of information. Many of the basic mathematics questions will be word problems, in which you are asked to make a calculation based on the information given in a short passage. We will look at a couple of sample word problems a little later in this section.

Multiple-Choice

Basic mathematics questions are in a multiple-choice format, with either four or five possible answers to choose from. When these answer choices are real numbers without variables, they will usually be listed in order from least to greatest. One exception to this rule is when a question concerns the relative value of the answer choices. For instance, in a question asking you to select the greatest of a group of fractions, the answer choices will be listed in a random order

Graphs, Charts and Geometric Figures

Some of the basic mathematics questions will include graphs, charts, or geometric figures. Unless the exam specifies so, these drawings will not be perfectly accurate and to scale. You should never make any assumptions about a diagram on the exam; only consider information that is either explicitly given by the question or that can be calculated based on information explicitly given.

Basic Math

Understanding What Is Asked

The most important thing to remember regarding basic mathematics questions is to read the question carefully and make sure you understand what it is asking. For instance, the exam is notorious for setting up an equation like $2x = 6$ and then asking you to solve for $x + 2$. Inevitably, many test takers will see the equation and simply solve for x; thus the exam punishes those who fail to read the question carefully. So, before you even begin to solve the problem or examine the answer choices, make sure you know what the directions are asking you to do.

On many of the basic mathematics questions, the exam will not require the highest level of specificity. For instance, when the answer to a problem is a decimal with nine places, the answer choices will often round to the nearest hundredth or thousandth. Before you go to the trouble of working out the problem to the millionths place, take a look at the answer choices: you may be able to save yourself some labor.

Scratch Paper

Although calculators are not allowed on the exam, scratch paper and pencils will be made available. You should use this scratch paper as much as you can. Do not try to solve complicated problems in your head; put them down on paper so that you can get a visual sense and leave your mind free to work. The importance of scratch paper is true for the data sufficiency questions as well as the basic mathematics questions, but on the basic mathematics questions you should use the paper to solve each problem forwards and backwards. For instance, on a question that asks you to solve for a specific variable, you should solve for the variable, then plug that variable back into the original equation and make sure that it works. After you have reviewed basic arithmetic and algebra, you should have plenty of time to work out problems forwards and backwards on your scratch paper. By double checking your work in this way, you can prevent careless mistakes from lowering your score.

Working Backwards

Let's consider an example of working backwards to solve a tricky basic mathematics question. Imagine that you are given the following scenario:

> *Brian takes an 81-inch piece of rope and cuts it three times. Each time he cuts the rope, he cuts off and discards the same fraction of the remaining length. When he is finished, the piece of rope is 3 inches long. Which fraction represents the amount of rope removed in each of the three cuts?*

This is a difficult question, and you may not know exactly how to approach it. This is when working backwards from the given answer choices can be an effective strategy. Let us imagine that the five answer choices for this problem are 1/8, 1/3, ½, 2/3, and ¾. When the answer choices are grouped in ascending order like this, it is a good idea to start with the middle value; if this answer is incorrect, you can often tell whether the right answer will be higher or lower.

So, returning to our example, let us begin with ½. If this is the correct answer, then the 3-inch rope left at the end of the problem would have been half the size of the rope remaining after two cuts. So, the amount of rope remaining after two cuts would be 6 inches. We can proceed on in this way: after one cut, the length of the rope would be 12 inches; before any cuts have been made, then, the length of the rope would be 24 inches. Obviously, since we know that the original length of the rope was 81 inches, ½ cannot be the correct answer. Furthermore, since plugging ½ into the problem yields an answer significantly smaller than we require, we can guess that the correct answer will be greater than ½.

Let us next consider 2/3, then. Remember that if 2/3 of the rope is cut off each time, the remaining amount will be 1/3 of the length before the cut. So, if the amount left after the third cut (3 inches) is 1/3 of the length of the rope before the third cut, the length of the rope before the third cut must be 9 inches (3 x 3 = 9). We can thus determine the preceding lengths of rope by multiplying by 3: before the second cut the length would have been 27 inches, and before the first cut, 81 inches. Aha! We can now be sure that 2/3 is the correct answer to the problem. Furthermore, we discovered this simply by working backwards from the answer choices given by the test.

ALGEBRAIC EQUATIONS

There are some basic mathematics questions, however, for which it is not prudent to work both forwards and backwards. This is true of problems in which working backwards would require too much time and effort. On these problems, it may be more efficient to set up a basic algebraic equation to derive the information you need. For instance, consider the following problem:

> *Vincenzo's Gourmet Coffee sells medium roast beans for $7 a pound and dark roast beans for $6 a pound. If Denise orders a 12-pound mixture that costs $6.25 per pound, how many pounds of dark roast beans is she getting?*

The answer choices for this problem are 3, 6, 8, 9, and 10. Certainly, it would be possible to solve this problem by working backward. If you chose 8 as your starting point, you could multiply by 6 and add the product (48) to the product of the amount of medium roast beans and their cost per pound (4 x 7 = 28). You could then add these two products together and divide by 12 to determine the cost per pound of Denise's mixture: (48 + 28)/12 = $6.33. This is the wrong answer.

Obviously, you would have to go to a fair amount of trouble to calculate the answer this way. For this reason, it is better to set up an algebraic equation using the information given in the problem. The variable x will represent the number of dark roast beans in the mixture. The amount of medium roast beans can therefore be represented as $12 - x$. We know that the total cost of the dark roast beans in the mixture, $6x$, added to the total cost of the medium roast beans in the mixture, $7(12 - x)$, can be divided by the number of pounds of the mixture, 12, to yield the cost per pound, which we know to be $6.25. In other words, we can set up the following equation to find the number of pounds of dark roast beans in the mixture: $[6x + 7(12 - x)]/ 12 = 6.25$. Multiply both sides by 12, and then multiply the 7 across the parentheses, yielding: $6x + 84 - 7x = 75$. Simplify and subtract 84 from both sides: $-x = -9$. Make both sides of the equation positive: $x = 9$. Of course, developing and solving this equation has its perils, but it is far less time-consuming and liable to careless error than working backward through a long series of calculations.

Geometric-Style Problems

Finally, a few of the basic mathematics questions on your exam will include geometric figures. Some geometry-style problems will not be accompanied by a figure, and it will be in your best interest to draw one of your own on scratch paper. In either case, remember that you can only trust information about the figure that is explicitly given. The exam will usually try to draw figures to scale, but it does not always succeed, so never make any assumptions about the relative sizes or angles of a figure. That being said, you can often derive some useful extra information from the values in the figure that are given. For instance, if you are given a square and told that one side is 6 inches long, you automatically know that all four sides are 6 inches long. Furthermore, you will know that every angle of the square is 90 degrees. This information may be required to find the answer to the problem.

Level of Difficulty

The basic mathematics section of the exam is broken down into three main content areas: arithmetic, algebra, geometry. The vast majority of the mathematics questions will require you to perform basic calculations with whole numbers, fractions, and decimals. As mentioned earlier, the level of difficulty of this section of the exam should not exceed an eleventh-grade level. What follows here is an outline of all the specific topics included in the exam. (Note: Do not try to read this section straight through! Either work through it paragraph by paragraph or use it as a reference for those topics that are unfamiliar or rusty. Space constraints prevent us from describing every topic exhaustively, so you may need to seek outside assistance on especially troublesome topics.)

Integers

Quite a few of the questions on the exam will require you to understand some of the basic properties of numbers, specifically integers. The set of numbers known as integers is composed of all the so-called counting numbers, both negative and positive, and including zero. So, expressed as a mathematical set, integers are {...-3, -2, -1, 0, 1, 2, 3,...}. Fractions and decimals are not integers. Any integer that is a multiple of two is called an even integer; all other integers are considered to be odd. Zero is considered to be an even integer. Zero has some special properties: any number multiplied by zero will yield a product of zero, and it is not possible to divide a number by zero. Any groups of integers that are arranged in order from least to greatest, and without any gaps, are referred to as consecutive integers.

Place Value

The value of an integer depends not only on the identity of the digits but on their placement. For instance, the numbers 0.61 and 0.061 are not the same. The position of a digit in a number is referred to as its place value. In order to answer some of the questions on the exam, you may need to be familiar with the more common place values. In a number that does not have a decimal point, the names of the place value increase by powers of ten as you move to the left. For instance, in the number 56,324, four is in the ones place, two is in the tens place, three is in the hundreds place, six is in the thousands place, and five is in the ten thousands place. It is easy to imagine how the progression of increasing places will continue: hundred thousands, millions, ten millions, etc. The place values on the right side of the decimal point also progress by powers of ten, beginning with tenths. As an example, in the number 0.5297, five is in the tenths place, two is in the hundredths place, nine is in the thousandths place, and seven is in the ten thousandths place. Again, it easy to imagine how these decreasing places will continue: hundred thousandths, millionths, ten millionths. Note that all of the place values to the right of the decimal point have a "th" at the end; make sure you don't confuse the thousands and the thousandths place on your exam.

Prime and Composite Numbers

Any number that can only be divided evenly by itself or one is a prime number. For example, three is a prime number because it can only be divided by three and one; four is not a prime number because it can be divided by two as well as by four and one. All numbers that are not prime numbers are referred to as composite numbers. Prime numbers are always positive, always whole numbers, and almost always odd (2 is the only even prime number).

Operations with Integers

Arithmetic is basically just performing operations with integers. There are a few things to remember when working with negative integers. A good rule of thumb is to remember that two negatives equal a positive: subtracting a negative number is the same as adding it; multiplying or dividing two negative numbers yields a positive product or quotient. On the other hand, when only one of the terms in a multiplication or division product is negative, the resulting product or quotient will be negative as well. When one integer cannot be divided evenly into another, the number that is left over is called the remainder. For example, in the problem $5 \div 2$, two can go into five two times, with a remainder of one; this is expressed 2 r 1.

Factors and Multiples

For any integer, the set of numbers that can be divided into that integer is known as its factors. Prime numbers will only have two factors: themselves and one. Composite numbers will have at least three factors: themselves, one, and some other number. The number 8, for example, has four factors: 8, 4, 2, and 1. The multiples of an integer are all of the values produced when the integer is multiplied by another integer. The multiples of 3 are 3, 6, 9, 12, and so on. The multiples of 4 are 4, 8, 12, 16, 20, and so on.

Associative and Distributive Properties

There are a few basic arithmetic properties which, although they are unlikely to be specifically mentioned on the exam, may help you to figure out some other problems. The associative property of addition asserts that the order of the terms in an addition problem does not matter, and so the various terms can be grouped and organized in any way without affecting the total. As an example, (2 + 5) + 6 = 13; and 2 + (5 + 6) = 13. Also, for that matter, 2 + 6 + 5 = 13, and 5 + 6 + 2 = 13. As long as the terms in an addition problem do not change, the sum will not change either.

In a similar vein, the associative property of multiplication asserts that the grouping of the terms in a multiplication problem will not affect the product. So, for example, 5 (2 x 3) = 30, 3 (2 x 5) = 30, 3 x 2 x 5 = 30, 5 x 2 x 3 = 30, and so on.

The distributive law is only slightly more complicated. It states that any number multiplied by a set of values within parentheses is multiplied by every value within the parentheses. To illustrate, 3 (5 + 4) = 3(5) + 3(4). Occasionally, the exam will ask you to transform a problem in the opposite way, as follows: 3(17) + 3 (14) = 3 (17 + 14). The problem may even be written in a slightly more confusing manner, such as: 5(12) – 83(5) = 5 (12 – 83).

Absolute Value

The absolute value of a number is its distance from zero. Absolute value is denoted by two vertical lines. Since absolute value is the measure of distance, it cannot be negative. So, the absolute value of 6, written |6|, is 6, and the absolute value of -6 is 6 as well.

Fractions

A fraction, for instance ½, consists of a numerator on top and a denominator on the bottom. Fractions are said to be equivalent when they can be reduced to be the same thing; for example, 5/10 is equivalent to ½, because it can be reduced to ½ by dividing both numerator and denominator by 5. Remember that when reducing a fraction you must divide numerator and denominator by the same number. In order to perform addition or subtraction operations with fractions, you must have a common denominator. Once you have a common denominator, you simply perform the operation with the numerators, leaving the denominators alone. To multiply two fractions, multiply the numerators together and then multiply the denominators together. To divide one fraction by another, invert the second fraction and then multiply first numerators and then denominators. A fraction in which the numerator is greater than the denominator is called an improper fraction. An expression consisting of a whole number and a fraction, for instance 5 ½, is called a mixed number.

Decimals

Decimals, like fractions, are a way of expressing values other than integers. Indeed, every fraction has an equivalent decimal: for instance, the fraction ¼ is equivalent to the decimal 0.25. When working with decimals, it is very important to understand how different operations affect the number of places to the right of the decimal point. When adding or subtracting decimals, the resulting sum or difference should have as many decimal places as the term in the operation with the most decimal places. In the problem 1.5 + 1.05, for example, the answer must have two numbers to the right of the decimal point. One way to simplify such problems is to add zeroes to the ends of those numbers with fewer decimal places; for instance, making our example 1.50 + 1.05. When two decimals are multiplied together, the resulting product will have the sum of the decimal places in the two terms. In other words, the product of 3.55 x 4.785 will have five places to the right of the decimal point, since the first term has 2 and the second term has 3. In order to divide decimals, the divisor must be converted into an integer by moving the decimal point to the right. So, in order to complete the problem 5.55 ÷ 2.8, we would need to shift the decimal point in both terms one place to the right, resulting in the problem 55.5 ÷ 28. The resulting quotient will have one place to the right of the decimal point.

Exponents

When the number is multiplied by itself several times, we use a form of notation called an exponent. For instance, the number 2^5 is expressed verbally as "two to the fifth power," and is equivalent to 2 x 2 x 2 x 2 x 2. When a number is raised to the second power (that is, when its exponent is 2), we say that the number is being "squared." When a number is raised to the third power (exponent is 3), we say that the number is being "cubed." For any number, an exponent of zero makes the number equal to 1. When the number has a negative exponent, is equal to one over the number raised to the absolute value of the exponent; in other words, $x^{-1} = 1/x$, $x^{-2} = 1/x^2$, $x^{-3} = 1/x^3$...

Operations with Exponents

There are specific rules for multiplying and dividing numbers with exponents. When two terms with the same base are multiplied together, as for example 2^3 x 2^4, the exponents are added together: 2^3 x $2^4 = 2^7$. When two terms with different bases but the same exponent are multiplied together, as in 2^3 x 3^3, only the two bases are multiplied: 2^3 x $3^3 = 6^3$. When the same base is given two exponents, as in $(3^2)^3$, the exponents are multiplied together: $(3^2)^3 = 3^6$. When two terms with the same base but different exponents are involved in a division problem, as in $3^4/3^2$, the exponent in the denominator is subtracted from the exponent in the numerator: $3^4/3^2 = 3^2$. Finally, when a fraction is given an exponent, as in $(3/4)^2$, the exponent applies to both the numerator and the denominator: $(3/4)^2 = 3^2/4^2$.

Square Roots

The number that when multiplied by itself would produce a given number is called the "square root" of that given number; for instance, 2 is the square root of 4, since 2 x 2 = 4. Note that -2 could also be considered a square root of 4, since -2 x -2 = 4. Every positive number will have two square roots, one of which will be negative. Also, since any positive or negative number multiplied by itself has a positive product, negative numbers do not have square roots. (This will probably not come up on the exam, but the square root of 0 is 0, since $0^2 = 0$). The standard notation for square root is $\sqrt{2}$, which is expressed verbally as "the square root of 2." If a question is specifically asking for the negative square root of 2, this is expressed $-\sqrt{2}$. When two square roots are multiplied together, the numbers are simply multiplied and the resulting product remains as a square root: $\sqrt{2}$ x $\sqrt{3} = \sqrt{6}$. In like fashion, when one square root is divided by another, the terms inside the root symbol are divided and the square root sign is left intact: $\sqrt{8}/\sqrt{4} = \sqrt{2}$.

Order of Operations

There is a specific order in which the various components of an arithmetic problem must be performed. This system is known as the order of operations, and is as follows: parentheses, exponents, multiplication, division, addition, and subtraction. The order of operations is easy to follow if you just remember the mnemonic phrase "Please excuse my dear Aunt Sally." The first letters of the words in this sentence (Please Excuse My Dear Aunt Sally) mirror those of the order of operations: Parentheses, Exponents, Multiplication, Division, Addition, and Subtraction. So, as an example, take a look at the following arithmetic expression: $3(4 + 3^2) - 2$. In order to derive the correct answer, you would need to begin by determining the value of the parentheses, first by calculating the exponent 3^2, and then by adding 4. Next, you would multiply by 3 (since multiplication preceded subtraction in the order of operations), and finally you would subtract 2. The correct value of this expression is 37. Note that if you tried to calculate the value of this expression without observing the proper order of operations (say, by subtracting 2 from the parentheses before multiplying by 3) you would not find the same answer.

Percents

When a number is expressed as a percentage, this means that it is being expressed as a portion of 100. So, 25% is equivalent to 25 hundredths, or 0.25. Another way to express this is as a fraction: 25/100. If you prefer, you can always convert the percentages on the exam into decimals or fractions. The most common kind of percentage problem you will see on the exam is one that asks you to find a certain percentage of the given number. These problems are easily solved by multiplying the decimal equivalent of the percentage by the given number. As an example, imagine you are asked to calculate 25% of 40; you would simply multiply 0.25 by 40, resulting in an answer of 10 (remember the rules for multiplying decimals!). A similar kind of question will ask you to determine what percentage of a given number another number is. For instance, a question might ask what percentage of 40 the number 8 is. The way to solve this kind of problem is to set up a proportional equation as follows: $8/40 = x/100$. This equation can be expressed as "8 is to 40 as x is to 100." Such an equation can then be solved by cross multiplying and solving for x, yielding an answer of 20%.

Ratios

Another name for the proportion on either side of the last percentage equation is ratio. A ratio is simply a comparison between numbers. Indeed, ratios are noted in the same way as verbal analogies, since both involve a consideration of the relationship between two things. The ratio 4 to 5, then, would be expressed 4:5. Ratios can also be expressed as fractions: for example, 4/5. Some ratios can be simplified. For instance, in the ratio 8:12, both terms are divisible by 4, so we can simplify the ratio to 2:3.

Basic Algebraic Operations

For the most part, performing operations with algebraic expressions is the same as performing operations with numbers. Remember that algebraic terms can only be combined when the variables are identical. This includes any exponent attached to the variable. For instance, the expression $6x^3 + 4x^2 - 2x^2 + 5x + 4x - 7$ can only be simplified to $6x^3 + 2x^2 + 9x - 7$, and an expression like $5x^2 + 4x - 3y^2$ cannot be simplified at all.

Some questions may ask you to factor a given algebraic expression. To factor an algebraic expression means to simplify it by breaking it down into its constituent components. One common form of algebraic expression is $x^2 - y^2$, which can be factored to become $(x + y)(x - y)$. This is true no matter what variable is used or what the value of x or y is, so for instance $z^4 - 16 = (z^2 + 4)(z^2 - 4)$.

Inequalities

In most algebraic equations, the two sides will be separated by an equal sign (=). Sometimes, however, the symbol will be one that indicates an inequality. There are five inequality symbols that can appear on the exam: <, meaning "is less than"; >, meaning "is greater than"; ≤, meaning "is less than or equal to"; ≥, meaning "is greater than or equal to"; and ≠, meaning "is not equal to." In almost every case, working with an inequality is the same as working with a normal equation (i.e., one with an = sign). The only exception is that when both sides of an inequality are multiplied by a negative number, the direction of the inequality reverses. So, the result of dividing -3 into both sides of the inequality $-6 > -3x$ would be $2 < x$.

Lines and Angles

The basic unit of geometry is the line. Unless it is specified otherwise, lines are assumed to travel in opposite directions infinitely. Lines that are finite are called line segments. Where two lines intersect, angles are formed. The exam will require you to know a few of the basic types of angles. A right angle is one in which the two sides of the angle are perpendicular to one another; a right angle measures 90°. An acute angle has a measure between 0° and 90°. An obtuse angle has a measure between 90° and 180°. An angle with a measure of 180° is called a straight angle, although for all intents and purposes this is just a straight line. Two or more angles that add up to 90° are referred to as complementary angles. Two or more angles that add up to 180° are referred to as supplementary angles. There is no such thing as a negative angle, or an angle measuring 0°. When two lines intersect and form 4 angles, the angles opposite one another are referred to as vertical angles; vertical angles are always equal. When two parallel lines (i.e., lines extending infinitely in either direction but never touching) are intersected by a third line, known as a transversal, the corresponding angles formed are called transverse angles.

Triangles

There are a few properties and varieties of triangles that you will need to know for the exam. In every triangle, the largest angle is opposite the longest side. The sum of the lengths of the two smallest sides of a triangle will be greater than the length of the longest side. When the measures of the angles inside a triangle are added up, the sum is always 180°. A triangle with three equal sides into three equal angles is known as an equilateral triangle. A triangle with two equal angles and two equal sides is referred to as an isosceles triangle. A triangle that has no equal sides and no equal angles is referred to as a scalene triangle. Any triangle in which one angle is equal to 90° is called a right triangle. In such a triangle, the two sides that form the right angle are called the legs, and the other side is called the hypotenuse. The Pythagorean Theorem describes one unique property of right triangles: the sum of the squares of the lengths of the two legs is equal to the length of the hypotenuse squared. The Pythagorean Theorem is usually written as follows: $a^2 + b^2 = c^2$. Remember that the Pythagorean Theorem only works for right triangles.

Quadrilaterals and Other Polygons

A quadrilateral is any figure with four sides, in which the four interior angles add up to 360°. There are a few special quadrilaterals. A quadrilateral with four equal sides and four right angles is called a square. A quadrilateral with four equal sides and four interior angles that are not equal is called a rhombus. A quadrilateral with four equal angles and two opposite and equal pairs of sides is called a rectangle. All the angles in a rectangle are right angles. A quadrilateral with two opposite and equal pairs of sides and two opposite and equal pairs of non-right angles is called a parallelogram. A quadrilateral with four unequal angles and one pair of parallel sides is called a trapezoid.

Triangles and quadrilaterals are the types of polygons (closed figures) you are most likely to encounter on the exam. You should know the names of some other regular polygons, however. A regular polygon is one in which all the sides and all the angles are equal. A regular polygon with five sides is called a pentagon. A regular polygon with six sides is called a hexagon. A regular pentagon with seven sides is called a heptagon. A regular polygon with eight sides is called an octagon. A regular polygon with nine sides is called a nonagon. A regular polygon with ten sides is called a decagon. There is a simple formula for determining the sum of the interior angles in a regular polygon: simply subtract two from the number of sides and multiply by 180°. The sum of the interior angles of a pentagon, for instance, would be $(5 - 2)\ 180° = 540°$. You can find the measure of each interior angle by dividing the sum of the interior angles by the number of sides in the figure: $540°/5 = 108°$.

Circles

In geometry, a circle is defined as all of the points in a plane that are the same distance from a given point (the center of the circle). The distance from the center of a circle to any point on its border is known as the radius. Any line that passes from one edge of the circle to another is called a chord. The length of a line extending from one edge of the circle to another and passing through the center is known as the diameter. The diameter is the longest chord in any given circle. The diameter of a circle is twice the radius. The distance around the edge of the circle is known as the circumference of the circle. The circumference of a circle can be determined with the following equation: $c = 2\pi r$, in which r is the radius of the circle. The set of points including and connecting any two points on the edge of the circle is called an arc of the circle. Like angles, arcs are measured in degrees; the largest possible arc is 360°. Any line that intersects with a circle in exactly one point is called a tangent of that circle. The radius running from the center of the circle to the point at which a tangent intersects the edge of the circle will be perpendicular to the tangent. Two or more circles that share a center but have different diameters are referred to as concentric circles.

Area and Perimeter

You will need to know a few basic formulae for calculating the area of various figures. The area of the triangle is calculated: *a* = ½*(base x height)*, where the base is one side of the triangle and the height runs perpendicular to the base. The perimeter of the triangle, and indeed the perimeter of any polygon, is the sum of the lengths of the sides. The area of a square, rectangle, or parallelogram can be calculated by multiplying the length by the width. The area of a rhombus can be calculated by multiplying one half by the product of the two diagonals (lines drawn between the vertices of opposing angles). The area of a circle is found: $a = \pi r^2$, in which r is the radius of the circle.

Cylinders, Rectangular Solids, and Cubes

Occasionally, the exam will require you to work with basic three-dimensional figures like cubes, cylinders, and rectangular solids. A cylinder (shaped like a can) has two parallel circular bases of equal diameter. The height of a cylinder is measured perpendicular to the bases. The surface area of a cylinder is measured with the equation $A = 2(\pi r^2) + 2\pi rh$, in which r is the radius of the bases and h is the height. The volume of a cylinder can be calculated with the equation $V = \pi r^2 h$. A rectangular solid (shaped like a box) has six faces and twelve edges, connected at eight vertices. The volume of a rectangular solid is calculated with the equation $V = lwh$, in which l is length, w is width, and h is height. If these three measures are equal, the rectangular solid is called a cube. The surface area of a rectangular solid is calculated with the equation $A = 2(wl + lh + wh)$; in other words, surface area is the sum of the areas of the six faces of the rectangular solid.

Coordinate Geometry

Coordinate geometry is the placement of points, lines, and figures on a coordinate axis. On the exam, you are only going to work with coordinate geometry on a plane: i.e., in two dimensions. The two dimensions of a plane are defined with an x-axis, which runs horizontally, and a y-axis, which runs vertically. These two lines intersect at the origin, and divide the place into four quadrants. The quadrants are numbered in a counterclockwise fashion, beginning with quadrant I in the upper right. Any point on the coordinate plane can be described with a pair of numbers, one indicating the point's placement on the x-axis, and one indicating the point's placement on the y-axis. All the values on the x-axis that are to the left of the origin are negative. All of the values on the y-axis that are below the origin are negative. The point at which a line intersects the x-axis is known as the x-intercept, while the point at which the line intersects the y-axis is known as a y-intercept.

More often than not, the coordinate geometry questions on the exam will be asking you to determine the slope of a line. These questions can take a couple of different forms. Some questions will tell you that a line passes through two given coordinates, and then will ask you to calculate the slope. In such a case, the slope can be found with the following equation: slope = rise/run, or slope = $(y_1 - y_2)/(x_1 - x_2)$.

Mean, Median, Mode

Some questions on the exam may present you with a set of data and ask you to name the mean, median, or mode of the set. The mean of a set is the same thing as the average, and is calculated in the same way, namely by adding together all the values in the set and dividing by the number of values in the set. For instance, then, in the set of data {5, 6, 4, 9}, the mean would be calculated as follows: (5 + 6 + 4 + 9)/ 4 = 6. The median of a set is the middle value when the set is arranged from least to greatest. So, in the set {1, 3, 5}, the median is 3. If the set contains an even number of values, the median is calculated by adding together the 2 middle values and dividing by 2. So, for the set {2, 4, 6, 8}, the median would be calculated: (4 + 6)/2 = 5. Finally, the mode of a set of data is the value within the set that occurs most frequently. Sometimes, a set will have more than one mode, or, if every value within the set appears only once, it will not really have a mode at all.

Range and Standard Deviation

For any given set of values, the range is the distance from the greatest value to the least. This can be calculated by subtracting the least value from the greatest. So, for the set {2, 5, 7, 8, 12), the range would be calculated 12 – 2 = 10. The method of calculating range is not affected by the number of values in the set, or by the number of values that share the least or greatest measure.

Calculating the range is a rather crude way of judging the dispersion of values in a set of data. A more sophisticated measure is standard deviation. The process of determining standard deviation has several steps. First, the arithmetic mean of the set must be calculated. Next, the difference between each member of the set and the arithmetic mean must be found, and these differences must be squared and added together. This sum is then divided by the number of values in the set, and the square root of the quotient is found. The standard deviation is the absolute value of this square root (since standard deviation cannot be negative). Although it is unlikely that you will be required to calculate the standard deviation for a set of data, you should still have a working knowledge of the method for calculating standard deviation. It is more typical for a question to give you the mean and the standard deviation of a set, and then to ask you to determine the range of a certain number of standard deviations from the mean. For example, say a set of data has a mean of 6 and a standard deviation of 2. If you are asked to calculate the range of values within 2 standard deviations of the mean, you can do so by first multiplying the standard deviation by 2. Standard deviation extends to either side of the arithmetic mean, so the range will be all the values within 4 on either side of the mean. In other words, the range of values within 2 standard deviations of 6 will be 2 through 10.

Average

The word *average* is synonymous with the word *median*. The basic rule for finding the average of a set of data is to add up all the members of the set and then divide by the number of members. The average of a set containing 1, 3, 6, and 6 would be calculated: (1 + 3 + 6 + 6)/4 = 4.

Some problems will give you the average of an incomplete set of data and ask you to identify the missing term. You can solve this kind of problem by rearranging the equation for finding an average. Instead of average = sum/# of members, use sum = average x # of members. So for instance, if you are told that the average of a set containing 7, 5, x, and 20 is 10, you can determine that the sum of the members of the set must be 10 x 4 = 40. Since the known members of the set add up to 32, the missing member of the set must be 8.

On rare occasions, you may have to deal with weighted averages, in which some of the values in the set are given more importance than others. For example, imagine that during the last ten games a certain baseball team scored 8 runs one time, 4 runs three times, 2 runs five times, and 0 runs one time. You could not simply add up 8, 4, 2, and 0 and divide by 4 to find the average number of runs scored over the last ten games. Instead, you need to set the number of members of the set as ten, and then multiply each value by its number of occurrences before adding. So, the average would be calculated as follows: [1(8) + 3(4) + 5(2) + 1(0)]/10 = 3.

Distance, Rate, and Time

Probably the most common type of word problem on the exam is the one that asks you to consider distance, rate, and time. You will recognize these problems; they begin with something like, "John drives 3 hours at 50 miles per hour. How many miles does John drive?" In other words, two values are given and you are asked to find the third. This is easy enough when you remember the simple equation *distance* = *rate* x *time*. In the example problem, the rate is 50 mph and the time is 3 hours, so the distance is 150 miles. Always make sure that the units in the problem are consistent, as you won't get very far trying to convert kilometers per hour into miles. Also, be aware that the unknown variable will not always be distance, in which case you will need to rearrange the equation to solve for rate or time. For instance, if the problem states that "Dale drives 75 miles at 25 miles per hour," and asks you to determine how many hours Dale has been driving, you will need to solve for t, and so your equation will be $t = d/r$. If the problem asks you to solve for rate, the equation will need to be rearranged to $r = d/t$.

Interest Problems

Some word problems will require you to calculate the amount of interest that accrues on a given amount of money over a certain amount of time. In order to solve these problems, you will need to know the equation $I = prt$, in which I is interest, p is principal, r is rate of interest, and t is time. Imagine the following scenario: $20 is placed into an account with an annual interest rate of 5%. How much interest will the money have accrued over 5 years? The principal is $20, the interest rate is 5% (for the purposes of calculation you will want to convert the percentage into a decimal, so 5% becomes 0.05), and the time is 5, so the equation can be set up: $I = 20 \times 0.05 \times 5$, yielding an answer of $5. Remember to make sure that if the interest rate is annual, the time needs to be in units of years as well (for instance, six months would become 0.5). Don't worry about compound interest or variable rates; the interest-related questions on the exam do not get so complex.

PROBABILITY

The exam will only cover the most basic concepts of probability. The essential formula to remember when dealing with these problems is that the probability of something occurring is equal to the number of outcomes in which the thing occurs divided by the total number of possible outcomes. For instance, imagine that you have a drawer full of ties, 7 of which are red and 5 of which are black. If you reach into the drawer and pull out one tie at random, the probability of selecting a red tie would be 7/12, and the probability of pulling out a black tie would be 5/12. Some questions will require you to combine probabilities. Using our example, we would say that the likelihood of selecting either a red or black tie would be 7/12 + 5/12 = 1. A probability of 1 means that the event is absolutely going to occur (conversely, a probability of 0 means that the event is definitely not going to occur); there is no such thing as a negative probability.

In some cases, you will be asked to determine whether two events are independent or mutually exclusive of one another. Two events are described as being independent of one another when the occurrence of one does not have any effect on the possible occurrence of another. For instance, there is a certain probability that the Dodgers will win the World Series, and there is a certain probability that a small meteor will crash into the Indian Ocean, but there is absolutely no connection between these two events, which are therefore said to be independent of one another. Events are defined as mutually exclusive when the occurrence of one makes it impossible for the other to occur. For instance, since the Dodgers and the Yankees cannot both win the World Series, these two events can be described as mutually exclusive.

GRAPHS

The graphs used on the exam will be of the kinds most familiar to students: circle/pie graph, double axis line graph, triple axis line graph, and bar graph. Remember that on a circle or pie graph, the circle itself represents 1 or 100%. A double axis graph, otherwise known as a line graph, has a horizontal and a vertical axis, each of which represent an individual variable. A triple axis graph has an additional vertical axis on the right side, which is used to mark a third variable. A bar graph is composed of vertical or horizontal bars representing certain values. In rare cases, a question may include two kinds of graph. When confronting this sort of problem, be sure that the units and scale used by the two graphs are consistent. If they are not, you will need to make adjustments in order to make accurate comparisons of data from each of the graphs.

Police Judgment

Purpose

In the line of duty, a state trooper has to make quick decisions. It is no exaggeration to say that the ability of the trooper to act appropriately can mean the difference between life and death. For this reason, state troopers undergo extensive training and must prove themselves to their superiors before they are given the full responsibilities of the badge. Nevertheless, even before you receive this training the state trooper entrance examination will require you to demonstrate the ability to use common sense and moral judgment to make a quick decision. Every version of the state trooper examination contains at least a few items testing your ability to select the appropriate response to a given situation.

Format

These questions come in a number of different formats. In perhaps the most common format, you will be given a hypothetical scenario and asked to choose the most effective response. Sometimes, these hypothetical situations will be preceded by a table of information that you must use to make your decision. For instance, an examination might provide you with a basic summary of common traffic violations. Then, the exam will describe some hypothetical scenarios and ask you to determine whether a violation has been committed. It is common for these hypothetical scenarios to contain irrelevant information designed to confuse you; be sure you restrict your decision-making process to the pertinent facts.

Judgment Exercise

In another common police judgment exercise, a fictional scenario will be outlined through the accounts of several witnesses. Each of these witnesses will be providing information from a unique point of view; their account of the situation may be incomplete or colored by their personal bias. It will be your job to determine what facts can be established and what should be the appropriate course of action. As a state trooper, you will often be forced to rely on imperfect accounts from fallible witnesses. You need to be able to sort out the believable information in a hurry and decide upon a course of action.

Minimum Force

Although you will not need to know specific police protocol in order to succeed on these questions, there are a few basic ideas that you can keep in mind to improve your performance. The first important concept is called the principle of minimum force, a principle which applies to all law enforcement work. The principle of minimum force simply states that the appropriate amount of force for a given situation is the least amount of force necessary to accomplish the goals of the officer. In other words, you should always use as little force as possible. The precise amount of force that is appropriate will depend on the situation, and you are not expected to know exactly what to do in every conceivable scenario on the written examination. However, a good rule of thumb is to always choose the answer in which the least amount of force is used and the goals of action are attained.

Helping People in Trouble

Of course, in order to determine the minimum amount of force you need to have an understanding of your intention. For instance, the amount of force required to immediately subdue every individual on the scene is probably more than would be required to protect the innocent. In order to determine appropriate action, then, you need to have a basic understanding of the priorities of a law enforcement officer. The number one priority of every law enforcement officer is to help people who are in trouble. This duty takes precedence over every other responsibility. So, if you were to witness a pedestrian being hit by a car, your first responsibility would be to determine the status of the victim. Only after making sure that the victim is taken care of should you begin to go after the driver.

Maintaining Peace

The second most important duty of a law enforcement officer is to maintain peace. In large part, state troopers exist not to prevent criminal activity but to preserve order in the community. Whenever a conflict between citizens exists, it is the duty of the officer to defuse it before it endangers life and property. When a situation is volatile, restoring peace is the officer's top priority after assisting injured individuals.

Enforcing Law

After assisting injured individuals and maintaining the peace, the next responsibility of the state trooper is to enforce the law. In other words, once a situation is under control and all the parties concerned are safe, you can turn your attention to violations that may have occurred. Of course, it may be necessary to restrain certain individuals in order to accomplish the first two priorities.

Assisting

The fourth responsibility of a state trooper is to help out anyone who needs help but is not in immediate danger. For instance, state troopers are obliged to assist elderly, handicapped, homeless, sick, and intoxicated people. Even though these people may not be in any particular danger, they are considered by the law to be vulnerable and therefore deserving of assistance from law enforcement officials.

Maintaining Order

Finally, if all of the above duties have been fulfilled or are not at issue, a state trooper's priority should be to maintain order in his or her domain. When you see state troopers patrolling a highway or neighborhood, they are usually just maintaining order. They may not have any particular purpose at the present time, but they know that establishing a presence on the streets and making observations will reduce crime and improve their ability to observe crimes being committed.

Emergency Situations

There is a slightly different set of priorities for emergency situations. In emergency situations, when the life of the state trooper or of an innocent civilian is in danger, the state trooper is allowed to act so as to protect himself or the innocent even if his or her actions violate orders. It is assumed that the state trooper will be able to justify his or her actions in violation of orders after the fact. When there is no immediate danger to the state trooper or to another innocent individual, the state trooper is required to follow orders. Assuming that he or she is following orders, the state trooper may also act to protect property and restore peace. However, state troopers should not perform any actions to protect property or restore peace if those actions violate explicit orders.

If you can keep the principle of minimum force and the priorities of a law enforcement officer in mind as you are thinking about these police judgment questions, you will have no trouble. On most of the items, all the information required to find the answer will be included in the question. Try to work methodically and take into account all of the pertinent information given in the passage. The exam may try to confuse you by including nonessential information; feel free to mark through this information with your pencil to remind yourself that it is not important. Be sure to read every answer choice carefully, and remember that for a state trooper the best move and the safest move are often one and the same.

Orientation

Purpose

Almost every state trooper examination will include some questions which require you to use a map. You need to become familiar with all highways and thoroughfares in your patrol area. At times, you may need to travel to a location outside of your normal zone and will need to use a map to find your way. Moreover, you may need to reach a certain location in a hurry and time cannot be wasted getting lost or going the long way. In addition, you may need to describe locations and give directions to colleagues, emergency personnel, and members of the community. To accomplish all of these tasks, you will need to be adept at reading a map and discerning the most appropriate path from one place to another.

Question Types

The orientation questions on the state trooper exam may appear under a number of different headings: map-reading, spatial orientation, and direction-finding are all names for the same type of question. Sometimes you will need to obtain information from the map, and sometimes you will need to use the information on the map to solve a problem. There are a few different ways that these questions may be designed. On one type of question, you'll be presented with a map and asked to chart the best directions from one place to another. Another question may simply ask you to identify the directional relationships between two locations; in other words, to state in which direction one location lies in relation to another location. These questions may involve using a map or following a brief set of written directions. In some orientation questions, you will begin in a certain location and follow a list of directions; after you have followed all of the directions, the question will ask you to describe your new location. Finally, you may be presented with a question that asks you to follow a set of directions and then describe which compass direction you end up facing.

Using Roadmaps

The maps that you encounter on the orientation section of the state trooper exam will almost always be roadmaps. When necessary, these maps will include a compass identifying north, south, east, and west. You will not need any familiarity with other types of maps in order to succeed on these questions. You will be allowed to rotate the map, which many people find helps them to gain the proper point of view. You are also allowed to draw lightly on the map with a pencil. Treat the map as you would the scratch paper during the mathematics section of the exam; write down your work as you go, so that you can clear your mind to consider the next step in the problem.

Determining Best Direction

When you are asked to outline the best directions from one point to another, remember that you must obey all traffic laws. Only in the most extreme emergencies are state troopers allowed to violate the law. For instance, you cannot recommend directions that force you to go the wrong way down a one-way street. In addition, remember to account for the features of different kinds of road. For example, the speed limit on a highway is generally much higher than it is on a residential street, and so in some cases it may be more efficient to go a slightly longer distance on the highway than to take the most direct route through a neighborhood. Many of the maps used on the state trooper examination will indicate the presence of traffic lights and stop signs; you should take these impediments into account when constructing your directions.

Practicing

There are a number of ways that you can practice for this part of the written examination. Perhaps the easiest and most beneficial way is to practice using a map in the real world. Obtain a map of the area close to where you live. Then pick a nearby location you have never visited before. Using the map, try to determine the most efficient route to this location. You can then hop in the car and try to follow your directions to the location without referring to a map.

If you are already confident in your ability to read a map and select the optimal directions, try testing yourself against one of the online map services. These websites use global-positioning system (GPS) technology and complex algorithms to analyze traffic patterns. They also take into account traffic laws and speed limits, and are therefore able to predict the fastest route with a high degree of accuracy. Using your own map, determine the best possible route between two locations. Then, enter the origin and destination into the online map service and see if you get the same results. If you are able to generate the same set of directions as the website, you are ready for the exam. If your directions vary considerably from those produced by the website, try to determine where you have gone wrong. Sometimes, you may decide that your directions are actually better than those produced by the map service. In particular, GPS-derived directions are often accused of failing to account for significant changes in elevation that will affect driving time. In any case, these online map services are a great way to hone your skills in preparation for the orientation questions on the state trooper written examination.

Imaginary Map Questions

Occasionally, you will be presented with an orientation question that is not accompanied by a map. These questions typically provide you with a set of directions which you must follow in your imagination. An example of this kind of question is as follows: "You drive 3 miles east on Maple Street, then turn and drive two miles north on Main Street. If you then drive four miles west on Cedar Avenue, where are you relative to your original position?" The most important step in solving a problem of this type is to use your scratch paper. If you are required to take units of distance into account, simply tear off a small scrap of paper and have this represents one unit. To solve our example question, then, you could draw a line 3 units east (to the right on your paper), and then draw a line two units long up from the end of the first line. Finally, draw a line four units long from the end of the second line to the left. The most appropriate answer to this question would thus be "northwest." Although these questions are somewhat rare on the state trooper written examination, you should practice a few of them before the exam day. Be sure to read the directions carefully and use your scratch paper, and you should have no trouble solving these problems.

Memory

Purpose

The state trooper written examination will contain a number of questions designed to test your memory. This is because accurate and detailed recall of information is a crucial part of success as a state trooper. In order to be effective in law enforcement, you have to be able to make intelligent observations and remember what you have observed. You will be drawing on your memory in the composition of reports, in the testimony you give in court and in your meetings with your superior officers. Moreover, your ability to make effective observations will depend on the strength of your memory. For instance, once you have become familiar with your patrol area, you should be able to observe any suspicious individuals or activity more easily. It is your memory of the usual state of affairs that enables you to notice things that are out of the ordinary.

Also, when a criminal incident occurs, you'll need to be able to provide detailed recollections of the people, events, and circumstances. If your memory is not reliable, it may be impossible to prosecute a criminal. Also, you may miss important observations that would enable justice to be served. For this reason, law enforcement departments deem it essential to only employ those officers with superior observation and recall skills.

Short-Term Memory Skills

The prospect of being tested on short-term memory skills is a daunting one for many state trooper applicants. Many people claim to have a poor memory for names or faces and believe that this deficiency cannot be remedied. The good news is that these people are wrong: every person can improve his or her memory by learning a few basic strategies and practicing. Essentially, memory is a matter of will power and habit; those individuals who make a point of remembering important details will find that they do so as a matter of course. In a bit, we will take a look at a few ways you can improve your short-term memory. First, though, let's take a brief look at the kinds of memory questions likely to appear on a state trooper written examination.

Realistic Scenarios and Tasks

The memory questions on state trooper written examinations do not waste time on superfluous matters; they tend to feature realistic scenarios and tasks. Most of these questions require you to study a photograph, drawing, passage of text, or set of data for a limited period of time and then recall information from it. For instance, a common memory question presents a license plate number for a brief period of time and then asks you to select the number from a list of five. During the completion of the memory questions, the exam administrator will sit with you and limit your perusal of the information to be remembered. You might receive 30 seconds to a minute for a photograph, or a couple of minutes for a passage of text.

Recalling Specific Details

One very common type of memory question asks you to examine a series of wanted posters. Each of these posters will contain a photograph and brief description of a criminal suspect. You will be given a few minutes to look over the series of wanted posters, and then you will be asked a set of questions based on them. The most common kind of question will ask you to recall specific details from the physical appearance or description of a given suspect. Another kind of question might draw a thumbnail sketch of an observed individual and ask you to determine which of the wanted suspects the observed individual most resembles. A question might ask you to name the type of disguise that would be most appropriate for a given suspect, or to choose the search method that would be most appropriate for a given subject. You will not be required to have any specific knowledge of police procedure to answer these questions; common sense will be the only requirement.

Another frequently used memory question format involves the presentation of a long, detailed passage, which you are given a few minutes to read. Once the allotted time is up, the passage is removed and you are required to answer a few questions. The questions may ask you to recall specific details from the passage, or to outline a possible plan of action based on the information in the passage. You are responsible for even the most minor details in the passage, so do your best to read carefully and thoroughly. Some of the memory strengthening techniques we will discuss below will prove helpful here.

Finally, state trooper written examinations often contain a photograph or illustration which you are allowed to study for a limited period of time before answering a series of questions. This picture may or may not depict criminal activity. You may be asked to recall specific details from the picture, to identify possible criminal activity in the picture, or simply to give a brief description of the pictures contents.

Remaining Calm

Whichever type of memory question you receive, it will be important for you to concentrate fully and remain calm. Studies consistently show that emotional stress and anxiety diminish memory. When the mind becomes agitated, it is incapable of retaining as much information in short-term storage as when it is relaxed. So, in order to maintain your calm during memory exercises, it is important for you to practice these types of items in the weeks and months before your exam. Moreover, targeted memory practice can actually increase your capacity for short-term storage. In other words, with a little practice anyone can become a memory master.

Mnemonic Strategies

Before we start looking at the particulars of police observation, let's consider a few basic principles of memory. To begin with, remember the distinction between short-term and long-term memory. Short-term memories are those which are kept present in the mind for a relatively brief period of time, whereas long-term memories are filed away and become a permanent part of the individual's remembrance. In the context of the state trooper written examination, you will primarily be tested on your short-term memory. The human mind has a limited capacity for short-term memory storage; in fact, attempting to store excessive amounts of information in short-term memory can actually diminish the overall capacity of short-term memory bank. For this reason, it is important to use a few basic mnemonic strategies to maximize the capacity of the short-term memory bank.

Associational Thinking

For one thing, you should know that most scientific studies declare that the average maximum number of sequential pieces of information that a person can store in short-term memory is seven. A phone number or a license plate number pretty much maxes out short-term memory. Therefore, in order to retain this information while making room in short-term memory for new information, you need to develop strategies for transferring memories from short-term to long-term storage. The best way to do this is through associational thinking. In a strict sense, all memory is associational: we only remember things that have significance because of their relation to other things. Most people tend to remember things that have to do with their own lives and the lives of those they care about; as an example, consider whether you would be more likely to remember the weather forecast for the region in which you live or the forecast for a country on the other side of the world. The human mind is conditioned to filter out nonessential information, which is basically defined as any information which does not relate to the individual in question.

This is a long way of saying that the best way to remember something is to consciously relate it to something you already remember. For instance, imagine you are introduced to a new coworker named Carl Smith. This is a fairly unmemorable name, and so you might employ a basic associational strategy in order to remember it. In your mind's eye, you might for example imagine Carl with a huge bushy beard, so that he looks like the German philosopher and economist Karl Marx. And now that you have that picture of Carl in your mind, you might imagine him forging iron on an anvil: in other words, being a Smith. This is just one (slightly silly) example of using associational thinking to create a mental picture and solidify memories. You can choose any images that are particularly memorable to you. The point is to connect new information to images and ideas you have already stored in long-term memory. This has the effect of shifting the new information into long-term storage, from which it can be recalled at any time.

You can apply this mnemonic strategy to any new information: sequences of letters and numbers, physical characteristics, names, and dates. Of course, the best way to make a memory concrete is to write it down as soon as possible, while the information is still fresh in your mind. As a state trooper, you'll need to make constant written notations of the things you observe. On the exam, however, you will have to maintain mental control of new information. You can use the associational strategy to improve your recall of seemingly random information.

Prioritizing Information

Just as important as learning *how* to remember is learning *what* to remember. The mind can receive and process huge amounts of information at once, but it needs to be able to discriminate between what is important and what is not. This ability to discriminate is even more essential for state troopers, who need to be able to rapidly ascertain whether dangerous or criminal activity is in progress. Observation, in other words, must be complemented by the intelligence and experience. Although you will not be tested on specific police procedure during the written examination, your performance on the memories section of the exam can be improved by learning the physical and other characteristics that are most important to remember.

Consider the example of a wanted poster. Most of the time, a short text description below the photograph or drawing will list the individual's physical characteristics. This description usually includes such basic information as height and weight, but it also makes a point of including any information which is unusual and therefore distinctive. As a law enforcement official, this is the sort of information you need to be looking for. For instance, when you look at a photograph of an individual, look for any tattoos, scars, or birthmarks. The sort of identifying characteristics can only be hidden by surgery and makeup, so they are most effective at identifying a suspect. Other features, like facial hair, clothing, and jewelry, are less reliable, because they can be easily changed. However, if a suspect does not know that he or she is being pursued, he or she is more likely to retain these changeable aspects of appearance. So, if a memory question asks you to examine a photograph of an individual or a wanted poster, be sure to concentrate your efforts on remembering the most unique and distinctive characteristics of the individual.

The necessity of prioritizing information applies to other kinds of memory questions. For instance, some memory questions will require you to look at an illustration of a potentially criminal situation. Before you begin committing the information in the picture to memory, take a moment to survey the entire picture and determine what is going on. If a picture contains several people, for instance, you should be able to guess the role of each individual. Not only will this help you remember their individual characteristics, but it will show you which people deserve the most attention. For obvious reasons, it is more important for you to remember the physical characteristics of an assailant that of a victim. With this in mind, try to figure out the story being told by the picture before you begin to focus on details.

Importance of Practice

Perhaps more than on any other section of the exam, your performance on the memory sections can be impeded by anxiety. Research continually suggests that stress diminishes the capacity of short-term memory. For this reason, it is especially imperative for you to practice these kinds of exercises so that you will be relaxed during the examination. An easy way to practice is to study a newspaper or magazine photograph and then have a friend ask you questions about it. You can perform a similar exercise with brief newspaper articles. The human memory is remarkably plastic; that is, it can improve in a short period of time with the right kind of stimulation. By practicing the kinds of exercises that will appear on the state trooper written examination, you can guarantee success on testing day.

Physical and Psychological Examinations

Physical Exam

Purpose

In order to be an effective state trooper, you need to possess both physical and mental strength. For this reason, state law enforcement departments include a brief physical examination as part of the application process. Applicants are not required to be in extraordinarily good condition during the application process; the law enforcement agency assumes that academy training will bring candidates up to the level required for service. Nevertheless, state trooper applicants need to be able to prove a minimum amount of physical ability in order to be considered for employment. Because it is time-consuming and expensive, the physical examination is usually performed relatively late in the application process.

Although the particulars of the physical examination vary from state to state, in general these assessments focus on those physical skills which will be most important for employment as a state trooper. The most demanding physical tasks performed by a state trooper will be sprinting and subduing suspects. Therefore physical strength, cardiovascular endurance, and the ability to perform brief and intense cardiovascular activity are the focus of the examination; flexibility and agility are less frequently tested.

Exam Specifics

A basic physical examination might include the following: a short sprint with obstacles; push-ups; sit-ups; and an extended run.

- *The short sprint with obstacles:* Designed to replicate the pursuit of a criminal on foot. The obstacles involved are typically no higher than the knees, though the course may require you to make several 90° turns. All of these features of the course are designed to mimic the obstacles encountered in an urban environment. Typically, state troopers are required to complete a 75-yard run in approximately 18 seconds.

- *Push-ups and sit-ups:* Provide a basic measure of the strength and endurance of the upper body and torso. Applicants are typically told to complete as many push-ups or sit-ups as they can within one or two minutes. In order for a push-up to be complete, the body must remain aligned and the elbows must first bend, lowering the body so that the nose touches the floor. The elbows must then extend until they are locked. A proper sit-up is performed with the fingers interlocked behind the head and the knees flexed at a 45° angle, with the feet together. The upper body is lifted by the contraction of the abdominal muscles; when the elbows touch the thighs, the abdominal muscles are relaxed until the mid-back touches the floor. A successful candidate should be able to perform at least 30 push-ups or 45 sit-ups in two minutes.
- *Extended run:* Designed to measure your cardiovascular endurance and stamina. This run is typically performed around a track, and it is one or two miles long. You should be able to maintain a steady jogging pace for the entire period. In general, a successful state trooper applicant will be able to cover 1.5 miles in less than 13 minutes.

State Requirements

This basic physical examination contains elements from all of the important fitness categories. However, it is possible that the state in which you are applying will have unique fitness requirements that necessitate special training. To find out the specific physical requirements for the state in which you are applying, visit the state trooper website. Most states post specific guidelines for the physical examination. In addition, many states publish training guides that outline how to prepare for the physical examination. These guidebooks often contain specific instructions for female candidates. Some states even offer free practice sessions so that applicants can get accustomed to the assessment procedures. Try to obtain as much information as possible about the physical examination performed in your state, and start training at least six weeks in advance of your examination. Exercise physiologists assert that it takes at least this long to register any significant gains in fitness.

Psychological Exam

Purpose

Most state trooper examinations contain some form of psychological assessment. This assessment is usually performed towards the end of the application process, for a couple of reasons. For one thing, psychological examinations are rather expensive, so the government tries to weed out inferior candidates before paying for the examination. Also, your performance in the other areas of the application process may indicate certain areas that need to be explored during the psychological examination. The psychological examination may contain written tests, individual interviews, or a mixture of the two. In it, you will be required to describe yourself, including your behavior, habits, personal history, and lifestyle. In general, these examinations are performed according to a state standard and by psychological professionals licensed by the state. The purpose of this examination is to ensure that you are a stable and psychologically healthy individual who will pose no risk to your fellow officers or to the public at large. A state trooper holds considerable power and has the potential to influence the lives of others in a major way; the state can be held liable for individuals who exercise this power in an unethical way. For this reason, the psychological examination seeks to determine whether you have any traits that could lead to problems on the job.

Honesty

Although there is not much you can do to prepare for a psychological examination, you can at least be aware of the issues that are of the most importance to the state examiners. Perhaps the most important trait that is analyzed in a psychological examination is *honesty.* As a state trooper, you will be depended upon to give honest testimony and to accurately describe events. Your ability to tell the truth will have an enormous impact on the lives of others. For this reason, the state examiner is obliged to ensure that you are a generally honest individual. The psychological examiner will ask you questions and study your responses, looking for any inconsistencies. Also, the examiner will compare your responses to the information obtained in a background search, to determine whether you are being truthful. It cannot be said forcefully enough: never lie during a psychological examination. Not only is your lie likely to be detected, but it will place you in an inconvenient situation for the remainder of your tenure as a state trooper. The fear of having a lie discovered can corrupt even the most ethical individuals. Besides, in most cases the offense you are trying to hide will be less serious than lying. There are many things that the psychological examiner will forgive; dishonesty is not one of them.

Substance Abuse

One of the more common areas in which your honesty will be tested is in the matter of prior and current substance abuse. The psychological examination will always include questions about your use of alcohol and other intoxicants. Moderate alcohol use is not a problem; though once you are hired the department will have strict rules regarding alcohol consumption. If you are currently abusing illegal substances, you are not fit to become a state trooper. Frankly, substance abusers will be unlikely to make it this far in the application process. Always assume that the background check will uncover everything there is to know about you. This will prevent you from lying or misrepresenting yourself to the examiner. Anyway, most state police departments do not make prior drug use an automatic disqualification. However, this information will be taken into account. Lying, on the other hand, will result in an automatic disqualification. If you have used drugs in the past, simply admit it to the examiner and indicate what you have learned and how your behavior has changed subsequently.

Equivocation

A more subtle area in which many applicants struggle during the psychological examination is the matter of equivocation. Equivocation is the practice of saying two things at once; in other words, making two arguments which are inconsistent with one another. Individuals often equivocate to avoid providing information about a subject they deem to be shameful or personal. In the context of everyday interactions, equivocation can be a harmless way of deflecting criticism or avoiding confrontation. During a psychological examination, however, equivocation indicates a willingness to manipulate the truth to advance a personal agenda. If the psychological examiner feels that you're equivocating rather than divulging crucial information, you will be penalized. For this reason, it is always to your advantage to answer the examiner's questions honestly and directly. Do not try to "spin" your answer.

Level of Stress

Some of the questions on the psychological examination will be designed to measure your general level of stress. The life of a state trooper is naturally full of stressful interactions, so the police department wants to eliminate candidates who have pre-existing problems with anxiety. The psychological examination will likely ask you to describe your strategies for handling difficult people and situations. Clearly, resorting to violence is not an acceptable way to resolve a stressful situation. Neither is screaming or threatening your antagonist. As a state trooper, you have to be able to control your temper and act according to police procedure. If the examiner feels that you have not developed healthy strategies for managing the ordinary stresses of life, he or she will not be confident in your ability to handle the extraordinary stresses of life as a state trooper. Angry candidates, or candidates who allow the job to affect their emotions to the detriment of their work, will be eliminated from consideration.

Indication of Growth

This brings us to a crucial element of the psychological examination: your indication of learning and psychological growth. During the examination, you should make a point of describing how you have learned from adverse situations in your past. If you have developed specific strategies for dealing with stress and loss, you should absolutely mention these during the examination. A psychological examiner will be very impressed by individuals who acknowledge their own insufficiencies and demonstrate the steps they have taken to mitigate the consequences of their errors. If you have not developed a specific strategy for dealing with life's struggles, you should give it some thought before your psychological examination. Basic relaxation techniques, like deep breathing and visualization training, will help you not only during the psychological assessment but during your subsequent career as a state trooper.

Hypochondria

A final character trait that can be diagnosed by the psychological examiner is hypochondria. Hypochondria is chronic complaining about poor health. In many cases, hypochondriacs complain about medical conditions which either do not exist or are not particularly severe. The state law enforcement department does not want to employ individuals who are constantly getting sick or demanding medical attention. Hypochondriacs not only put a financial strain on the medical insurance department, but they are a liability to their coworkers. Now, this does not mean that you cannot complain about legitimate conditions: just be sure that any medical complaints you make during the psychological examination can be validated by subsequent medical examination.

Clean Living

Psychological examiners always say that the best preparation for an examination is clean living; if you have nothing to hide, you will have no trouble giving clear answers that satisfy the examiner. Of course, not everyone can walk into the psychological examination with a squeaky clean conscience. For most people, there is some trepidation about having past indiscretions discovered. Nevertheless, you should resolve to participate in the examination with honesty and forthrightness, as this attitude will go a long way towards ensuring a positive report.

Optimal Mental Health

To this end, you should do your best to be in optimal mental health at the time of the exam. In general, the best preparation for the psychological examination is a good night of sleep and relaxation during the assessment. As much as possible, you want to convey to the examiner that you are comfortable with yourself, both your strengths and weaknesses. The psychological examiner is not trying to find perfect individuals, but rather to ensure that state troopers have developed healthy and mature systems for managing their own behavior. Your goal during the psychological examination should not be to avoid admitting your past mistakes or lapses in judgment; it should be to describe how you dealt with these mistakes in the past and have tried to deal with them since.

Oral and Medical Examinations

Oral Examination

Purposes

In addition to the psychological examination, most state trooper applicants are required to sit for an oral examination in front of a board of certified examiners. The members of the board will be experts and officials from state governments, particularly from the field of law enforcement. Their job is to ensure that you have the interpersonal skills required to function effectively as a state trooper. State troopers are expected to maintain cordial and civil relationships with their coworkers and the community in which they serve. Numerous studies have shown that a positive relationship between law enforcement professionals and the community tends to diminish crime. Moreover, state troopers who have built good relationships in the community are better able to apprehend criminals and obtain useful information.

The purpose of this oral examination, then, will be slightly different than that of the psychological examination. Whereas the psychological examination is designed to identify and examine any personal issues that may adversely affect your performance as a state trooper, the oral examination assesses your ability to represent the department in a positive manner in public. The oral examination is more like a traditional job interview, and you can expect to receive questions about your interest in law enforcement and your personal philosophy of professionalism. Oral examinations are usually recorded so that they can be studied in more depth at a later date. Also, the examining department likes to keep a copy on hand in case any disputes arise in the future.

Making a Good Impression

Perhaps the most important thing you can do to ensure your success on the oral examination is make a good first impression. Be sure to dress nicely for your interview; a suit and tie for males and a formal dress suit for females are appropriate in most cases. Most law enforcement departments recommend business attire for the oral examination. Make sure that your clothing is ironed and pressed. Before you say a word, the examiners will be judging you based on your personal appearance: clean clothes and proper grooming indicate your ability to represent the department in a positive manner.

When you enter the examination room, introduce yourself to all of the board members. Try to remember the names and ranks of the people who are interviewing you. If you can refer to these individuals by name and rank (as for instance, "Officer Jenkins") rather than as "Sir" or "Madam," you will demonstrate your professionalism and respect for seniority. This will go a long way to curry favor with the examiners. Also, when you are introducing yourself, give a firm handshake and maintain eye contact with the person you are meeting. You want to appear confident and sure of yourself without indicating superiority or cockiness.

Try to remember your past interactions with state troopers: no doubt you will have observed that the best troopers are those who project strength without patronizing or diminishing other people.

Describing Yourself

At the beginning of the oral examination, you will probably be asked to describe yourself. Before you enter the examination room, you should work out a basic biographical summary for the beginning of the interview. Describe your family background, your education, your military or professional experience, and any personal interests or hobbies that relate to your desire to become a state trooper. Remember that the purpose of this description is to indicate why you are best suited to become a state trooper, and not to exhaustively cover every significant event in your life. Restrict yourself to those events and achievements that have direct bearing on your career choice. However, do not exclude any hugely important events that do not seem to have direct significance to your application. For instance, if you are a cancer survivor, it is important to describe this struggle to the examiners, as an example of your persistence and ability to triumph over adversity.

Lines of Questioning

Once you have briefly summarized yourself, the board of examiners will ask you a series of questions. Although the questions will vary depending on the state and the particular interview, you can be assured that you will be asked why you want to become a state trooper. "I don't know" is not an acceptable answer to this question. If you have not fully articulated to yourself your reasons for becoming a state trooper, you need to do so before entering the examination room. Serving the public, contributing to an orderly society, and giving something back to the community are all great reasons for becoming a state trooper. In addition, it is appropriate to mention the professional perks of becoming a state trooper: good pay, excellent benefits, and a positive work environment. These more self-serving reasons, however, should not be the first thing you mention. It is important that you have the right motivations for becoming a state trooper, as this ensures that you will maintain the highest standards of ethical practice when you are on the job.

- *Hypothetical situations:* Another common line of questioning is one in which you are presented with a hypothetical situation and asked to describe the best response. The situations presented through these questions are similar to those found in the police judgment section of the written examination. For instance, the examiners might describe a car accident in which several of the drivers and passengers are wounded, and ask you to describe the protocol for alerting paramedics and assigning blame for the accident. You will not need to know the specifics of police training in order to answer these questions; rather you will need to demonstrate an appreciation for the importance of safety and a general amount of common sense. In large part, these questions are asked not to obtain a specific answer, but so that the examiners can gauge your ability to think on your feet. Candidates who cannot provide any answer or provide a confusing answer will be penalized. Candidates who demonstrate the ability to reason through a problem and produce a thoughtful solution will be rewarded.
- *Ethics:* An oral examination may also include specific questions about ethics. The panel may ask you questions about your own personal conduct, and about the standards for professional conduct that you expect to follow as a state trooper. Before you sit for the oral interview, you should bc familiar with the code of ethics that applies to state troopers. Any racist, sexist, or homophobic language is forbidden. The expression of any opinions which explicitly violate the code of ethics may result in your immediate elimination as a candidate. As with the psychological examination, you do not want to lie about your past conduct during the oral examination; however, it is appropriate for you to suggest how you have learned from your mistakes and how you plan to act in the future. The board of examiners will be looking for evidence that you are capable of taking instruction and making ethical decisions on your own.

Ask Questions

After the board of examiners has concluded their set of questions, you'll probably be asked if you have any questions of your own. You should have at least one question to ask the panel. Asking the panel questions about life as a state trooper indicates that you are interested and engaged; not having a question suggests that you are uninterested and uninformed. For this reason, you should prepare a few questions for the board before you enter the examination room. You can ask about issues of professional conduct, hypothetical situations, or even the specifics of the application process. In order to make a good impression on the examiners, you'll need to demonstrate your desire to be an engaged, informed, and passionate member of the department.

Body Language

Throughout the interview process, you can improve your performance by maintaining good posture and making eye contact with every member of the panel. As much as possible, try to eliminate verbal tics ("um," "uh," and "you know," for example). Practice your responses to common questions with a family member or friend, and have him or her critique your performance. Remember that your purpose in the oral interview is to present yourself as a positive future member of the state trooper department. Every word and gesture should reinforce your confidence, strength, and competence.

Medical Examination

Purpose

Before you can be admitted into the state trooper academy, you will need to pass a comprehensive medical examination. Law enforcement agencies need to have healthy employees who will not miss a great deal of work and will be able to fulfill the physical requirements of employment. Also, the state wants to limit the amount of disability and health insurance benefits it has to pay, so it is important to weed out unhealthy individuals during the application process. Finally, the law enforcement agency wants to ensure that you do not have any health conditions which would cause you to retire early from service.

Vision

The exact procedure for conducting the medical exam varies from state to state. In some states, it is acceptable to be examined by your regular physician; other states require you to be examined by a doctor employed by the state. In either case, the doctor will be instructed to examine you in certain specific areas. For one thing, the doctor will be required to check your vision. Imperfect vision is not an automatic disqualification from employment, although seriously impaired vision may inhibit your ability to perform the duties of a state trooper. In most states, applicants are required to have at least 20/25 vision when corrected (this means that you are allowed to wear glasses or contact lenses).

Hearing

The medical examination will also include testing of your hearing ability. Most law enforcement agencies measure hearing with an audiometer, which gauges your ability to clearly hear all of the normal tones in the human register. If your hearing has been impaired, you may need to seek treatment or electronic hearing aids in order to be considered for employment.

Drug Test

Besides these tests of vision and hearing, a medical examination will certainly include a drug test. As mentioned above, prior drug use does not necessarily disqualify you from employment. However, recent use of hard drugs will seriously diminish your likelihood of being hired. Being a drug user is simply not compatible with being a state trooper. If you are on any prescription medication that may affect your performance on a drug test, be sure to notify the physician before submitting blood or urine.

Overall Health

The remainder of the medical examination will likely include a dental exam, chest x-ray, complete blood count, and general physical assessment. These procedures are performed to determine whether or not you have any existing medical conditions which could inhibit your ability to perform your duties as a state trooper. Law enforcement agencies typically do not have requirements regarding height and weight, although your physical dimensions may prohibit you from certain types of work. Also, extremely overweight or underweight individuals may be scrutinized carefully during the physical examination. Some law enforcement departments prohibit smoking, and may include a test for tobacco use in the medical examination.

Background Check

Unless you have specific and serious problems in your background, you should not be too alarmed by the prospect of a comprehensive background check. A high proportion of background checks uncover no serious problems. Nevertheless, there is no harm in getting all of your references and personal data in order before beginning the state trooper application process. Make sure that your friends and family know you are applying to become a state trooper, so that they will not be surprised or disturbed if and when they are contacted by investigators. Remind them to tell the truth no matter what. If your background check uncovers any problematic information, immediately take the appropriate action and own up to your mistakes. Ultimately, the investigators will be most impressed by those candidates who demonstrate a willingness to take responsibility for their actions.

Purpose

Before your application to become a state trooper is complete, you can be sure that a full background check will be performed on you. The state department will use its own resources and outside sources to obtain information about your past relationships, financial history, and personal records. The comprehensive background check is one reason why you should never lie during the oral and psychological examinations; any essential information you attempt to hide will be uncovered during the background check. Because the background check is an expensive process, it is only performed on candidates who have reached the final stages of the application process and are likely to be accepted. The purpose of the background check is to ensure that you have consistently met a high ethical standard in your personal conduct, and that you do not have any personal issues that might hinder your performance as a state trooper. Although you might think there is nothing you can do to prepare yourself for a background check, this is not quite true. There are a few odds and ends you can take care of in advance of the application process to ensure that you make the best possible impression to the investigators.

Credit Check

The most important thing you can do to avoid trouble during the background check is to recognize any potential problems and do everything possible to defuse their impact. The state department will investigate several aspects of your life; we will take a look at them individually. To begin with, the state department will take a close look at your financial history. The most important aspect of this inquiry will be your credit rating, which is derived from your history of paying your debts on time. Believe it or not, credit rating is actually pertinent to performance as a state trooper. To begin with, an individual with a solid credit rating is more likely to be responsible and attentive to his or her duties. Staying current on your credit card or mortgage payment indicates that you fulfill your responsibilities and take care of your business. Furthermore, individuals who have money trouble may be more susceptible to bribes or appropriating money found during a drug bust or other criminal investigation. When officers are found to be obtaining money by these illegal means, it's a major public relations headache for the whole department (not to mention a criminal offense by the officers in question). The state department wants to make sure that it hires individuals who are relatively comfortable financially, so that they will not be tempted to obtain money unethically.

With this in mind, try to improve your credit rating as much as possible before you begin the state trooper application process. You can do this by getting current on your credit card payments, car payments, or mortgage. If you are unsure of what you as an individual need to do to improve your credit rating, you should see a financial professional. There are numerous online rating services which will provide you an estimated credit rating free of charge. It is a good idea to check your credit rating online even if you are certain you have no problems. Moreover, if you have not established credit, you may want to consider doing so before beginning the application process. Most state departments assert that a positive credit rating is an important component of a successful candidate profile.

Personal Relationships

The state department will also investigate your personal relationships. They will obtain information about your family members and spouse from public records, but they may also interview your friends and relatives. Many departments will require you to provide specific character references to fulfill this part of the background check. The individuals questioned as part of the background check for a state trooper application are required by law to tell the truth. Any failure to divulge pertinent information under direct questioning can be punishable. It is quite common for the state department to make inquiries to an applicant's spouse, siblings, parents, friends, and teachers. So, you may want to alert these individuals to the possibility that they will be contacted by investigators. Under no circumstances should you tell these individuals to lie on your behalf; rather, assure them that they can help you the most by being honest with the investigators.

Personal Habits

For the most part, the state department will be making these inquiries into your personal habits to determine if you have any characteristics which might impede your performance as a state trooper. Specifically, the investigators will be looking for evidence of substance abuse, gambling problems, marital discord, and other conflict. Law-enforcement agencies feel that all of these issues have the potential to undermine the performance of their officers. For instance, officers with gambling problems may experience wild fluctuations in income which make them vulnerable to bribes. Officers undergoing marital turmoil may become depressed and have their performance diminish. As noted above, prior substance abuse is not necessarily an automatic disqualification from service. However, lying about prior substance abuse will result in automatic disqualification. The same is true of other personal issues. The best strategy is always to be up front, acknowledging your problems and indicating how you plan to solve them.

Education and Professional History

Investigators will also take a look at your education and professional history. They may ask you to provide transcripts from your high school and post-secondary schools, and may require standardized test scores as well. If you do not have an extensive work history, investigators may require you to provide references from school. Try to select teachers who have worked with you personally, and who can vouch for your character as well as your academic skill. It is not necessary to be the world's greatest student in order to become a state trooper; however, the hiring agency will want to ensure that you take your studies seriously and that you have a fund of general knowledge.

Job History

The investigators will also take a look at your job history. They will use the information provided in your resume, and may contact your former employers for references. Obviously, it will not look good if you have been fired several times or if you have changed jobs frequently. The expense of training new state troopers is quite large, and the law enforcement agency will not want to waste this training on individuals who are likely to seek different employment in the near future. Basically, the hiring agency wants applicants who have decided to become state troopers for life. If you have changed jobs a number of times, you will want to provide an explanation. It may be that there is a perfectly good reason for this constant transition; at the very least, you want to assure the investigators that you intend to have a long career as a state trooper.

Criminal Record

Finally, you can be sure that the investigators will take a close look at your criminal record. If you have been convicted of several misdemeanors or a felony, you may be automatically disqualified from becoming a state trooper. However, in some situations candidates with a significant criminal record may be offered employment. If you have a problematic criminal record, you should immediately visit an attorney. He or she will be able to advise you as to the effect of your criminal record on your prospects of becoming a state trooper. Whatever your situation, under no circumstances should you attempt to hide past transgressions. There are a few things you can do to rectify minor problems, however. If you feel that you may have some unpaid parking tickets, contact the relevant office and make sure you are up to date. The same advice applies to any unanswered summons; make sure that you have complied with any official requests that have been made. If you are required to make alimony payments, make sure that you are current at the time of your application. Failure to pay alimony or child support will seriously diminish your chances of being hired as a state trooper.

Conclusion

As you can see, the state trooper examinations do not just measure one particular skill. Unlike other entrance examinations, which focus on a specific area of expertise, the state trooper examinations evaluate academic, physical, and interpersonal skills. This is because success as a state trooper depends on having this entire repertoire. The life of a state trooper is in constant flux: one day you may be interacting with the community, while another day you may be up to your ears in paperwork. In order to be a good employee, you will have to fulfill all of these divergent responsibilities with competence.

To this end, the state trooper examinations probe your mental, physical, and psychological abilities. Only those candidates who will represent the department to the community in a positive light will be selected. Remember, however, that the state trooper examinations are entrance exams: they predict whether you can succeed in the training academy and then as a professional state trooper. In other words, you will not be expected to have all of the skills and knowledge of a trained officer. On the contrary, the state law enforcement agency wants you to be eager and receptive to the comprehensive training you will receive in the academy. For this reason, your primary objective during the examination process should be to indicate your potential and your willingness to learn. Showing the exam administrators that you take the application process seriously and have made an effort to prepare will go a long way towards ensuring your success. Try to remain confident yet humble, and remember that the best way to relieve anxiety about the examination is to learn about it and prepare for it. We hope this guidebook will be a helpful companion as you start on the path towards public service and professional success as a state trooper.

CPR Guidelines for Professional Rescuers

Topic	Adult	Child	Infant
	Past puberty	**1 y/o - puberty**	**Under 1 y/o**
Conscious Choking	abdominal thrusts (or chest thrusts in pregnant/obese)	abdominal thrusts	5 back slaps and 5 chest thrusts in infant
Unconscious Choking	Begin chest compression. Look in the victim's mouth for foreign body before giving breaths.		
Rescue Breaths Normal breath given over 1 second until chest rises.	10-12 breaths per minute (1 breath every 6-8 seconds)	12-20 breaths per minute (1 breath every 3-5 seconds)	20 breaths per minute (1 breath every 3 seconds)
Chest Compressions to Ventilation Ratios (Single Rescuer)	30:2		
Chest Compressions to Ventilation Ratios (Two Rescuer)	30:2	15:2	
Chest Compression rate	At least 100/minute		
Chest Compression Land Marking Method	two hands center of the chest, even with nipples	one hand center of the chest even with nipples	2 or 3 fingers, just below the nipple line at the center of the chest
Chest Compression Depth	At least 2" compression (hands overlapping)	about 2" compression or 1/3 the AP diameter (only heel of one hand)	about 1 ½" compression or 1/3 the AP diameter (2 fingers)
Activate Emergency Response System	As soon as you realize that the victim is unresponsive	After 5 cycles of CPR	After 5 cycles of CPR

Checklist:

- Check the scene
- Check for responsiveness – ask, "Are you OK?"

- Adult - call 911, <u>then</u> administer CPR
- Child/Infant – administer CPR for 5 cycles, <u>then</u> call 911
- Open victim's airway and check for breathing
- Two rescue breaths should be given, 1 second each, and should produce a visible chest rise
- If the air does not go in, reposition and try 2 breaths again
- Check victim's pulse – chest compressions are recommended if an infant or child has a rate less than 60 per minute with signs of poor perfusion
- Continue 30:2 ratio until victim moves, AED is brought to the scene, or professional help arrives

Basic Class E Driving License Practice Test

Use your own state's driving license guide to assist you with answering the following questions. Most states' regulations in regards to traffic and driving are very similar. Consequently, the following information and correct answers may vary slightly between states. These questions were chosen to represent an overview of the driver's responsibilities on the road.

1. Which of the following is not required when getting started with the Driving Exam monitored by the instructor?

a. Adjust the seat
b. Make sure the car is in the park or neutral gear
c. Check the oil level under the hood
d. Fasten seat belt
e. Adjust the inside and outside mirrors for proper vision

2. Which of the following child weights is correct to require a Rear Facing Car Seat?

a. 20 lbs. to 2 yrs.
b. 40 lbs. to 3 yrs.
c. Birth to 15 lbs.
d. Birth to 20 lbs.
e. 3-4 yrs. old

3. Vehicle Condition relates to the following except:

a. Brake lights status
b. Tail lights status
c. Steering involving less than 3 inches of play in the wheel is safe
d. Tires with less than 1/16 tread are probably unsafe
e. All of the above are correct

4. All of the following comments related to Driver Safety are true except:

a. Drowsiness is the second step in falling asleep at the wheel
b. Drive looking 10-15 seconds ahead
c. Take in the whole scene
d. There are 2 blind spots to the left and right (back sides) of your car
e. Partial hydroplaning starts at 35 mph in wet conditions on the road

5. If passing a parked car watch for which of the following?

a. Smoke from the tailpipe
b. Red Brake lights on
c. White Backing Lights on
d. Only A & B
e. A, B, & C

6. Stopping Distance depends on all of the following except:

a. Your reaction time
b. Condition of the brakes
c. Condition/type of tires
d. Wind resistance
e. Road conditions

7. If you were traveling at 55 mph how far would an average car travel using the Stopping Distance eye to brain to foot to wheel to road guide in total distance?

a. 131 feet
b. 175 feet
c. 200 feet
d. 228 feet
e. 453 feet

8. If you were traveling at 35 mph how far would an average car travel using the Stopping Distance eye to brain to foot to wheel to road guide in total distance?

a. 52 feet
b. 76 feet
c. 106 feet
d. 129 feet
e. 270 feet

9. When turning around on a narrow street you should use the __ principle?

a. three point
b. Y
c. four point
d. A & B
e. B & C

10. If parking on a hill facing uphill you should do the following except:

a. Turn the wheels away from the curb
b. Turn the wheels toward the curb
c. Shift into low gear
d. Shift into park
e. Set the emergency brake

11. Which of the following Parallel Steps is not correct?

a. Signal
b. Stop parallel to the front car, approx. 3 feet from it
c. Back slowly
d. The front/rear bumper must be 2 feet from the other vehicles.
e. Use approximately a 45 degree angle from the street with backing up.

12. Lower headlights must be in use if within __ feet of an approaching vehicle or __ feet if following another vehicle.

a. 1000, 500
b. 2000, 400
c. 750, 300
d. 500, 200
e. 400,100

13. What percent of motorcycle/car accidents are the result of a car driver turning in front of a motorcyclist?

a. 25%
b. 33%
c. 66%
d. 75%
e. 90%

14. Pedestrians have the right of way in which of the following situations?

a. Walking within a marked crosswalk.
b. When crossing an intersection with a green traffic signal.
c. Over a vehicle making a right turn on red.
d. A&C
e. A, B, & C

15. Which of the following is correct?

a. Blind or partially blind pedestrians have the right of way.
b. Pedestrians should always walk against the flow of traffic.
c. Motorcycles are allowed the full width of a lane in which to maneuver.
d. A, B, & C
e. A & C

16. When it is against the law to pass another vehicle?

a. Within 200 feet of a bridge
b. The solid yellow line in your lane
c. Within 100 feet of an intersection
d. A, B, & C
e. B & C

17. Passing a vehicle should be completed before coming within __ feet of any vehicle approaching from the opposite direction.

a. 50 feet
b. 75 feet
c. 100 feet
d. 150 feet
e. 200 feet

18. You cannot pass a bus unless it is in an loading/unloading zone completely off the road or the road is divided by the following:

a. Ditch
b. Grassy Median
c. Elevated Concrete Barrier
d. Only B & C
e. All of the above

19. When approaching and turning through an intersection, which of the following are correct statements?

a. Finish the turn in the proper lane
b. You may use the left arm with signaling
c. Must get into the proper lane 150 feet before making the turn
d. A & B
e. A & C

20. It is legal to do the following:

a. Signal another vehicle to pass you with a turn signal
b. Turn around on a hill where your vehicle cannot be seen by other drivers approaching from either direction within 400 feet
c. Position the left arm straight for a left turn
d. A & B
e. All of the above

21. The right-of-way belongs to the following:

a. Emergency vehicles, pull over and slow down.
b. Emergency vehicles, pull over and stop.
c. The driver to the right arriving simultaneously at a stop sign with another driver has the right-of-way.
d. A & B
e. B & C

22. In which of the following situations is it legal to parallel park?

a. In front of driveway
b. Greater than 20 feet away from a fire hydrant
c. Greater than 15 feet away from of a crosswalk at an intersection
d. On a bridge, overpass, or in any tunnel
e. Greater than 30 feet away from a railroad crossing

23. When approaching a railroad crossing the following rules must be observed except:

a. Stop if the signal device is flashing and a train is approaching.
b. Stop if the crossing gate is lowered
c. Stop if the train gives a warning
d. Stop no less than 10 feet away from the nearest rail
e. Stop within 50 feet of a railroad crossing if the crossing gate is lowered.

24. Railroad crossing markings are the following:

a. White markings painted in the traffic lane before railroad crossings.
b. Pavement marked with a large "X" and two "R's".
c. There is a no passing zone.
d. A & B
e. All of the above.

25. Drivers of the following vehicles must stop at railroad crossings:

a. Drivers of vehicles carrying passengers for hire
b. School buses or trucks
c. Any vehicle carrying explosives
d. All of the above
e. B & C

26. All of the following are true regarding safety near a railroad crossing except:

a. Never shift gears on a railroad crossing
b. Never drive around any crossing gate a railroad crossing
c. Always look both ways as you approach a railroad crossing
d. A sign above the crossbuck indicates the number of track
e. A second train could be coming from the other direction

27. Which of the following is false regarding additional traffic laws?

a. Having non-transparent material upon the window glass of any vehicle is unlawful
b. Riding in a horse trailer is allowed while on a state highway
c. It is against the law for more than 3 persons to occupy the front seat of a moving vehicle.
d. Backing up is not permitted on any shoulder or roadway of any controlled-access highway.
e. Don't open your door on the traffic side unless it is clear to do so.

28. Which of the following is false regarding additional traffic laws.

a. Cannot follow closer than 1000 feet to an emergency vehicle that is responding to a call
b. Do not cross any unprotected fire department hose unless consent is given by an official of the fire department.
c. Littering in Louisiana can result in a fine not less than $100.
d. Coasting down a hill in neutral gear is illegal
e. You must not drive a vehicle that is overloaded with passengers or any thing that will obstruct your view in any direction or interfere with your control of the vehicle.

29. All of the following apply to interstate driving, choose the following statement that is false.

a. Traffic on the interstate has the right-of-way.
b. If you miss your exit, do not back up, do not stop.
c. If you stop on the side of the road turn on your 2-way emergency lights.
d. If you stop on the side of the road at night use flares or reflectors if broken down.
e. Do not stop in the acceleration lane unless traffic is too heavy and there is no space for you to enter safely.

30. If stopping in an emergency situation do all of the following:

a. Push the brake pedal hard
b. As the car begins to skid, quickly let up on the brake
c. Use a quick pumping action until the car is stopped
d. A & B
e. All of the above

31. If approaching an oncoming car in your lane you should do the following:

a. Blow your horn and flash lights, if you have time.
b. Do not drive into the left lane
c. Brake fast, but don't lock your wheels.
d. A & B
e. All of the above

32. If a passing vehicle is in danger you should do the following:

a. If it continues to attempt to pass, slow your vehicle and move to the right as far as you can with safety.
b. If the other driver definitely cannot complete the pass and must drop back, increase your speed.
c. If the right shoulder is safe, and a collision is almost certain, move quickly onto the shoulder to allow the passing car to move into your lane.
d. A & C
e. All of the above.

33. The following are all proper procedures to recover from a skid except:

a. Don't use the brakes
b. Take your foot off the gas pedal
c. Turn left for a skid to the left
d. Turn right for a skid to the left
e. Be careful not to over steer

34. If you run off the pavement you should do the following except:

a. Slow down by using your brakes only.
b. If there is no drop-off from the pavement steer back easily onto the road.
c. Turn back sharply onto the pavement checking traffic only in your lane.
d. A and C
e. All of the above.

35. If a tire blowout occurs you should do the following except.

a. Hold the steering wheel firmly
b. Attempt to move to the right traffic lane
c. Let your car slow down.
d. Don't use the brakes until you have slowed to a safer speed
e. Brake gently and pull all the way off the road into a safe area

36. If the brakes fail you should do the following except:

a. Pump the brake pedal slowly
b. Shift to a lower gear
c. Look for an escape route
d. Use your horns and lights as a warning to other drivers
e. Apply the parking brakes slowly

37. If the presence of fire appears near your vehicle you should do the following except:

a. Drive off the road clear of traffic and stop.
b. Turn off the engine and all electrical switches.
c. Get all passengers out of and away from the vehicle.
d. Attempt to open the radiator cap to let the radiator cool.
e. Seek assistance if a large gasoline or oil fire develops.

38. When jumping a dead battery you should do the following except:

a. Take off the vent caps from both batteries. Put a cloth over the open vent wells.
b. Turn on the lights, heater and radio.
c. Connect the positive post of the dead battery to the positive post of the dead battery.
d. Connect the negative post of the live battery to the negative post of the dead battery, or to the engine block or frame.
e. Take off the cables in reverse order.

39. If a breakdown occurs at night you should put flares at least ___ feet behind your car on the side of the road.

a. 50 feet
b. 100 feet
c. 150 feet
d. 200 feet
e. 300 feet

40. If a breakdown occurs during the day all of the following are acceptable except:

a. Using a white cloth and tying it to the radio antenna
b. Tying a red cloth to the left door handle
c. Raising the hood as a signal your car has broken down
d. It is generally best to wait outside your car in a safe place and stay with your car.
e. Be wary of strangers approaching your vehicle.

41. If you are involved in an accident, you are responsible to do the following:

a. Identify yourself
b. Required to give name, address, and vehicle license number if requested
c. Notify your insurance company.
d. A & B
e. All of the above

42. If you are not trained in first aid remember the following except:

a. To stop bleeding, place a clean cloth over the wound.
b. Ask a walking injured person to sit or lie down on his back.
c. If a person is bleeding from the lower part of the face or jaw, turn him on his side.
d. With serious injuries, improper movement may be harmful.
e. Attempt to transport an injured person to the hospital immediately in all cases.

43. Which of the following statements about alcohol is false?

a. Once alcohol enters the blood there is nothing you can do to lessen the effect
b. Alcohol affects you differently at different times.
c. Loss of caution and self-control is often the result of alcohol.
d. Alcohol can blur vision, increase reaction time and create a false feeling of confidence.
e. You cannot hide Drunk Driving.

44. Which of the following statements is false?

a. Marijuana will make the simplest task seem hopelessly confusing.
b. Marijuana will affect your eyesight.
c. Prescription drugs may make you drowsy and affect the control of your car.
d. Never use drugs and alcohol at the same time.
e. None of the above statements are false, all are true.

45. If you are under 21 and test positive for alcohol the following level must be attained to considered a DWI.

a. .01 per cent or more by weight of alcohol in your blood
b. .02 per cent or more by weight of alcohol in your blood
c. .05 per cent or more by weight of alcohol in your blood
d. .10 per cent or more by weight of alcohol in your blood
e. .20 per cent or more by weight of alcohol in your blood

46. If you are 21 or older and test positive for alcohol the following level must be attained to considered a DWI.

a. .01 per cent or more by weight of alcohol in your blood
b. .02 per cent or more by weight of alcohol in your blood
c. .05 per cent or more by weight of alcohol in your blood
d. .10 per cent or more by weight of alcohol in your blood
e. .20 per cent or more by weight of alcohol in your blood

47. Your driving privileges may be suspended for the following except:

a. Conviction of a DWI
b. Failing to answer a traffic law charge
c. Failure to comply with financial responsibility law when required
d. Any felony committed when operating a motor vehicle
e. All of the above may result in a loss of driving privileges

48. Your driving privileges may be suspended for the following except.

a. Failure to stop or passing a school bus loading or unloading children
b. Manslaughter or negligent homicide from the operation of a motor vehicle
c. Altering information on the license
d. Committing an offense in another state which, if committed in this state would be grounds for suspension or revocation
e. All of the above may result in a loss of driving privileges

49. If you refuse to submit to the test for alcohol your driving privileges will be suspended for __ days on your first offense.

a. 90 days
b. 180 days
c. 240 days
d. 300 days
e. 545 days

50. Vehicular Homicide is punishable by a fine not less than ___ dollars, nor more than ___.

a. 1,000; 7,000
b. 2,000; 15,000
c. 3,000; 20,000
d. 4,000; 25,000
e. 5,000; 30,000

Answer Key and Explanations

1. C

2. D

3. C

4. A

5. E

6. D

7. D

8. C

9. D

10. B

11. B

12. D

13. C

14. E

15. D

16. E

17. C

18. E

19. D

20. C

21. E

22. B

23. D

24. E

25. D

26. D
27. B
28. A
29. C
30. E
31. E
32. E
33. D
34. C
35. B
36. A
37. D
38. B
39. B
40. B
41. E
42. E
43. D
44. E
45. B
46. A
47. E
48. E
49. B
50. B

Basic Class D Driving License Practice Test

1. The maximum height for listed vehicles is ___.

a. 12'6"
b. 13'6"
c. 14'6"
d. 15'6"
e. 16'0"

2. A load must not extend more than __ feet to the front of the vehicle, or more than __ feet to the rear of the vehicle except poles, piling and logs.

a. 2,4
b. 3,5
c. 4,6
d. 4,8
e. 5,10

3. Poles, piling and logs may project ___ feet beyond the rearmost part of the trailer.

a. 5
b. 6
c. 10
d. 15
e. 17

4. If a load extends for 4 or more feet past the bed or body of any vehicle, a ___ flag 12 inches square must be attached to the extreme rear of the load during daylight hours.

a. red
b. white
c. blue
d. green
e. yellow

5. At night, a red light must be attached to the extreme rear of the load and visible for at least ___ feet to the sides and the rear.

a. 100
b. 200
c. 300
d. 400
e. 500

6. When pulling or towing another motor vehicle the speed limit is __ m.p.h.

a. 35
b. 45
c. 55
d. 60
e. 65

7. On a rural highway, drivers of motor trucks must not follow within __ feet of one another except to pass.

a. 200
b. 300
c. 400
d. 500
e. 600

8. Also, high beam headlights must be dimmed no less than ___ feet from oncoming traffic, and __ feet of a vehicle being followed.

a. 600, 200
b. 500, 200
c. 400, 200
d. 300, 100
e. 200, 150

9. Vehicles transporting passengers for hire must be equipped with at least a __ type fire extinguisher.

a. 1-A
b. 2-B
c. 1-AB
d. 2-BC
e. 1-A-B

10. Passenger buses and freight carrying vehicles must carry all of the following except.

a. Three flares
b. Two 12-inch square red cloth flags
c. Three electric lanterns
d. A & B
e. All of the following are required

11. Trucks carrying explosive, flammable liquid, compressed gases or using compressed gas as a fuel must use ______ or _______ only.

a. 2 12-inch square red cloth flags, three electric lanterns
b. 2 12-inch square red cloth flags, three flares
c. red electric lanterns, red emergency reflectors
d. red electric lanterns, white emergency reflectors
e. white electric lanterns, white emergency reflectors

12. If your brakes should fail on the level road, you should ______, and use engine compression to slow down.

a. up-shift
b. downshift
c. put on the emergency brake
d. throw out the anchor
e. accelerate

13. A rear view mirror must reflect a view of the highway for a distance of __ feet to the rear regardless of the load of the vehicle.

a. 100
b. 200
c. 250
d. 300
e. 350

14. Tail lights must be visible for __ feet to the rear.

a. 250
b. 500
c. 750
d. 1,000
e. 1,250

15. Reflectors must be visible for __ feet.

a. 200
b. 300
c. 450
d. 550
e. 600

Answer Key and Explanations

1. B

2. D

3. D

4. A

5. E

6. B

7. C

8. B

9. D

10. E

11. C

12. B

13. B

14. D

15. E

How to Overcome Test Anxiety

Just the thought of taking a test is enough to make most people a little nervous. A test is an important event that can have a long-term impact on your future, so it's important to take it seriously and it's natural to feel anxious about performing well. But just because anxiety is normal, that doesn't mean that it's helpful in test taking, or that you should simply accept it as part of your life. Anxiety can have a variety of effects. These effects can be mild, like making you feel slightly nervous, or severe, like blocking your ability to focus or remember even a simple detail.

If you experience test anxiety—whether severe or mild—it's important to know how to beat it. To discover this, first you need to understand what causes test anxiety.

Causes of Test Anxiety

While we often think of anxiety as an uncontrollable emotional state, it can actually be caused by simple, practical things. One of the most common causes of test anxiety is that a person does not feel adequately prepared for their test. This feeling can be the result of many different issues such as poor study habits or lack of organization, but the most common culprit is time management. Starting to study too late, failing to organize your study time to cover all of the material, or being distracted while you study will mean that you're not well prepared for the test. This may lead to cramming the night before, which will cause you to be physically and mentally exhausted for the test. Poor time management also contributes to feelings of stress, fear, and hopelessness as you realize you are not well prepared but don't know what to do about it.

Other times, test anxiety is not related to your preparation for the test but comes from unresolved fear. This may be a past failure on a test, or poor performance on tests in general. It may come from comparing yourself to others who seem to be performing better or from the stress of living up to expectations. Anxiety may be driven by fears of the future—how failure on this test would affect your educational and career goals. These fears are often completely irrational, but they can still negatively impact your test performance.

Elements of Test Anxiety

As mentioned earlier, test anxiety is considered to be an emotional state, but it has physical and mental components as well. Sometimes you may not even realize that you are suffering from test anxiety until you notice the physical symptoms. These can include trembling hands, rapid heartbeat, sweating, nausea, and tense muscles. Extreme anxiety may lead to fainting or vomiting. Obviously, any of these symptoms can have a negative impact on testing. It is important to recognize them as soon as they begin to occur so that you can address the problem before it damages your performance.

The mental components of test anxiety include trouble focusing and inability to remember learned information. During a test, your mind is on high alert, which can help you recall information and stay focused for an extended period of time. However, anxiety interferes with your mind's natural processes, causing you to blank out, even on the questions you know well. The strain of testing during anxiety makes it difficult to stay focused, especially on a test that may take several hours. Extreme anxiety can take a huge mental toll, making it difficult not only to recall test information but even to understand the test questions or pull your thoughts together.

Effects of Test Anxiety

Test anxiety is like a disease—if left untreated, it will get progressively worse. Anxiety leads to poor performance, and this reinforces the feelings of fear and failure, which in turn lead to poor performances on subsequent tests. It can grow from a mild nervousness to a crippling condition. If allowed to progress, test anxiety can have a big impact on your schooling, and consequently on your future.

Test anxiety can spread to other parts of your life. Anxiety on tests can become anxiety in any stressful situation, and blanking on a test can turn into panicking in a job situation. But fortunately, you don't have to let anxiety rule your testing and determine your grades. There are a number of relatively simple steps you can take to move past anxiety and function normally on a test and in the rest of life.

Physical Steps for Beating Test Anxiety

While test anxiety is a serious problem, the good news is that it can be overcome. It doesn't have to control your ability to think and remember information. While it may take time, you can begin taking steps today to beat anxiety.

Just as your first hint that you may be struggling with anxiety comes from the physical symptoms, the first step to treating it is also physical. Rest is crucial for having a clear, strong mind. If you are tired, it is much easier to give in to anxiety. But if you establish good sleep habits, your body and mind will be ready to perform optimally, without the strain of exhaustion. Additionally, sleeping well helps you to retain information better, so you're more likely to recall the answers when you see the test questions.

Getting good sleep means more than going to bed on time. It's important to allow your brain time to relax. Take study breaks from time to time so it doesn't get overworked, and don't study right before bed. Take time to rest your mind before trying to rest your body, or you may find it difficult to fall asleep.

Along with sleep, other aspects of physical health are important in preparing for a test. Good nutrition is vital for good brain function. Sugary foods and drinks may give a burst of energy but this burst is followed by a crash, both physically and emotionally. Instead, fuel your body with protein and vitamin-rich foods.

Also, drink plenty of water. Dehydration can lead to headaches and exhaustion, especially if your brain is already under stress from the rigors of the test. Particularly if your test is a long one, drink water during the breaks. And if possible, take an energy-boosting snack to eat between sections.

Along with sleep and diet, a third important part of physical health is exercise. Maintaining a steady workout schedule is helpful, but even taking 5-minute study breaks to walk can help get your blood pumping faster and clear your head. Exercise also releases endorphins, which contribute to a positive feeling and can help combat test anxiety.

When you nurture your physical health, you are also contributing to your mental health. If your body is healthy, your mind is much more likely to be healthy as well. So take time to rest, nourish your body with healthy food and water, and get moving as much as possible. Taking these physical steps will make you stronger and more able to take the mental steps necessary to overcome test anxiety.

Mental Steps for Beating Test Anxiety

Working on the mental side of test anxiety can be more challenging, but as with the physical side, there are clear steps you can take to overcome it. As mentioned earlier, test anxiety often stems from lack of preparation, so the obvious solution is to prepare for the test. Effective studying may be the most important weapon you have for beating test anxiety, but you can and should employ several other mental tools to combat fear.

First, boost your confidence by reminding yourself of past success—tests or projects that you aced. If you're putting as much effort into preparing for this test as you did for those, there's no reason you should expect to fail here. Work hard to prepare; then trust your preparation.

Second, surround yourself with encouraging people. It can be helpful to find a study group, but be sure that the people you're around will encourage a positive attitude. If you spend time with others who are anxious or cynical, this will only contribute to your own anxiety. Look for others who are motivated to study hard from a desire to succeed, not from a fear of failure.

Third, reward yourself. A test is physically and mentally tiring, even without anxiety, and it can be helpful to have something to look forward to. Plan an activity following the test, regardless of the outcome, such as going to a movie or getting ice cream.

When you are taking the test, if you find yourself beginning to feel anxious, remind yourself that you know the material. Visualize successfully completing the test. Then take a few deep, relaxing breaths and return to it. Work through the questions carefully but with confidence, knowing that you are capable of succeeding.

Developing a healthy mental approach to test taking will also aid in other areas of life. Test anxiety affects more than just the actual test—it can be damaging to your mental health and even contribute to depression. It's important to beat test anxiety before it becomes a problem for more than testing.

Study Strategy

Being prepared for the test is necessary to combat anxiety, but what does being prepared look like? You may study for hours on end and still not feel prepared. What you need is a strategy for test prep. The next few pages outline our recommended steps to help you plan out and conquer the challenge of preparation.

Step 1: Scope Out the Test

Learn everything you can about the format (multiple choice, essay, etc.) and what will be on the test. Gather any study materials, course outlines, or sample exams that may be available. Not only will this help you to prepare, but knowing what to expect can help to alleviate test anxiety.

Step 2: Map Out the Material

Look through the textbook or study guide and make note of how many chapters or sections it has. Then divide these over the time you have. For example, if a book has 15 chapters and you have five days to study, you need to cover three chapters each day. Even better, if you have the time, leave an extra day at the end for overall review after you have gone through the material in depth.

If time is limited, you may need to prioritize the material. Look through it and make note of which sections you think you already have a good grasp on, and which need review. While you are studying, skim quickly through the familiar sections and take more time on the challenging parts. Write out your plan so you don't get lost as you go. Having a written plan also helps you feel more in control of the study, so anxiety is less likely to arise from feeling overwhelmed at the amount to cover.

Step 3: Gather Your Tools

Decide what study method works best for you. Do you prefer to highlight in the book as you study and then go back over the highlighted portions? Or do you type out notes of the important information? Or is it helpful to make flashcards that you can carry with you? Assemble the pens, index cards, highlighters, post-it notes, and any other materials you may need so you won't be distracted by getting up to find things while you study.

If you're having a hard time retaining the information or organizing your notes, experiment with different methods. For example, try color-coding by subject with colored pens, highlighters, or post-it notes. If you learn better by hearing, try recording yourself reading your notes so you can listen while in the car, working out, or simply sitting at your desk. Ask a friend to quiz you from your flashcards, or try teaching someone the material to solidify it in your mind.

Step 4: Create Your Environment

It's important to avoid distractions while you study. This includes both the obvious distractions like visitors and the subtle distractions like an uncomfortable chair (or a too-comfortable couch that makes you want to fall asleep). Set up the best study environment possible: good lighting and a comfortable work area. If background music helps you focus, you may want to turn it on, but otherwise keep the room quiet. If you are using a computer to take notes, be sure you don't have any other windows open, especially applications like social media, games, or anything else that could distract you. Silence your phone and turn off notifications. Be sure to keep water close by so you stay hydrated while you study (but avoid unhealthy drinks and snacks).

Also, take into account the best time of day to study. Are you freshest first thing in the morning? Try to set aside some time then to work through the material. Is your mind clearer in the afternoon or evening? Schedule your study session then. Another method is to study at the same time of day that you will take the test, so that your brain gets used to working on the material at that time and will be ready to focus at test time.

Step 5: Study!

Once you have done all the study preparation, it's time to settle into the actual studying. Sit down, take a few moments to settle your mind so you can focus, and begin to follow your study plan. Don't give in to distractions or let yourself procrastinate. This is your time to prepare so you'll be ready to fearlessly approach the test. Make the most of the time and stay focused.

Of course, you don't want to burn out. If you study too long you may find that you're not retaining the information very well. Take regular study breaks. For example, taking five minutes out of every hour to walk briskly, breathing deeply and swinging your arms, can help your mind stay fresh.

As you get to the end of each chapter or section, it's a good idea to do a quick review. Remind yourself of what you learned and work on any difficult parts. When you feel that you've mastered the material, move on to the next part. At the end of your study session, briefly skim through your notes again.

But while review is helpful, cramming last minute is NOT. If at all possible, work ahead so that you won't need to fit all your study into the last day. Cramming overloads your brain with more information than it can process and retain, and your tired mind may struggle to recall even previously learned information when it is overwhelmed with last-minute study. Also, the urgent nature of cramming and the stress placed on your brain contribute to anxiety. You'll be more likely to go to the test feeling unprepared and having trouble thinking clearly.

So don't cram, and don't stay up late before the test, even just to review your notes at a leisurely pace. Your brain needs rest more than it needs to go over the information again. In fact, plan to finish your studies by noon or early afternoon the day before the test. Give your brain the rest of the day to relax or focus on other things, and get a good night's sleep. Then you will be fresh for the test and better able to recall what you've studied.

Step 6: Take a Practice Test

Many courses offer sample tests, either online or in the study materials. This is an excellent resource to check whether you have mastered the material, as well as to prepare for the test format and environment.

Check the test format ahead of time: the number of questions, the type (multiple choice, free response, etc.), and the time limit. Then create a plan for working through them. For example, if you have 30 minutes to take a 60-question test, your limit is 30 seconds per question. Spend less time on the questions you know well so that you can take more time on the difficult ones.

If you have time to take several practice tests, take the first one open book, with no time limit. Work through the questions at your own pace and make sure you fully understand them. Gradually work up to taking a test under test conditions: sit at a desk with all study materials put away and set a timer. Pace yourself to make sure you finish the test with time to spare and go back to check your answers if you have time.

After each test, check your answers. On the questions you missed, be sure you understand why you missed them. Did you misread the question (tests can use tricky wording)? Did you forget the information? Or was it something you hadn't learned? Go back and study any shaky areas that the practice tests reveal.

Taking these tests not only helps with your grade, but also aids in combating test anxiety. If you're already used to the test conditions, you're less likely to worry about it, and working through tests until you're scoring well gives you a confidence boost. Go through the practice tests until you feel comfortable, and then you can go into the test knowing that you're ready for it.

Test Tips

On test day, you should be confident, knowing that you've prepared well and are ready to answer the questions. But aside from preparation, there are several test day strategies you can employ to maximize your performance.

First, as stated before, get a good night's sleep the night before the test (and for several nights before that, if possible). Go into the test with a fresh, alert mind rather than staying up late to study.

Try not to change too much about your normal routine on the day of the test. It's important to eat a nutritious breakfast, but if you normally don't eat breakfast at all, consider eating just a protein bar. If you're a coffee drinker, go ahead and have your normal coffee. Just make sure you time it so that the caffeine doesn't wear off right in the middle of your test. Avoid sugary beverages, and drink enough water to stay hydrated but not so much that you need a restroom break 10 minutes into the test. If your test isn't first thing in the morning, consider going for a walk or doing a light workout before the test to get your blood flowing.

Allow yourself enough time to get ready, and leave for the test with plenty of time to spare so you won't have the anxiety of scrambling to arrive in time. Another reason to be early is to select a good seat. It's helpful to sit away from doors and windows, which can be distracting. Find a good seat, get out your supplies, and settle your mind before the test begins.

When the test begins, start by going over the instructions carefully, even if you already know what to expect. Make sure you avoid any careless mistakes by following the directions.

Then begin working through the questions, pacing yourself as you've practiced. If you're not sure on an answer, don't spend too much time on it, and don't let it shake your confidence. Either skip it and come back later, or eliminate as many wrong answers as possible and guess among the remaining ones. Don't dwell on these questions as you continue—put them out of your mind and focus on what lies ahead.

Be sure to read all of the answer choices, even if you're sure the first one is the right answer. Sometimes you'll find a better one if you keep reading. But don't second-guess yourself if you do immediately know the answer. Your gut instinct is usually right. Don't let test anxiety rob you of the information you know.

If you have time at the end of the test (and if the test format allows), go back and review your answers. Be cautious about changing any, since your first instinct tends to be correct, but make sure you didn't misread any of the questions or accidentally mark the wrong answer choice. Look over any you skipped and make an educated guess.

At the end, leave the test feeling confident. You've done your best, so don't waste time worrying about your performance or wishing you could change anything. Instead, celebrate the successful completion of this test. And finally, use this test to learn how to deal with anxiety even better next time.

Review Video: Test Anxiety
Visit mometrix.com/academy and enter code: 100340

Important Qualification

Not all anxiety is created equal. If your test anxiety is causing major issues in your life beyond the classroom or testing center, or if you are experiencing troubling physical symptoms related to your anxiety, it may be a sign of a serious physiological or psychological condition. If this sounds like your situation, we strongly encourage you to seek professional help.

Online Resources

Due to our efforts to try to keep this book to a manageable length, we've created a link that will give you access to all of your online resources:

mometrix.com/resources719/statetrooper

It's Your Moment, Let's Celebrate It!

Share your story @mometrixtestpreparation